Social Studies
for
Multiple Intelligences

Table of Contents

Multiple Intelligences G4–6, SV 9780547625744

Introduction

The Theory of Multiple Intelligences

In 1983, Howard Gardner introduced the theory of multiple intelligences in *Frames of Mind: The theory of multiple intelligences.* Gardner argued that the prevailing view of intelligence focused heavily on linguistic and logical-mathematical intelligences and often did not recognize other types of intelligences that students may possess. His theory of multiple intelligences identifies eight basic types of intelligence.

- Verbal-Linguistic intelligence
- Bodily-Kinesthetic intelligence
- Musical-Rhythmic intelligence
- Intrapersonal intelligence
- Logical-Mathematical intelligence
- Visual-Spatial intelligence
- Interpersonal intelligence
- Naturalist intelligence

Each type of intelligence can be viewed as a potential pathway to learning. Most students will have one or two dominant intelligences, but these intelligences are not used in isolation. Students will often use a combination of intelligences to complete a task or activity. Providing students with lessons that appeal to different types of intelligences can help students more easily learn and retain information.

Intelligence	Strengths	Activities
Verbal-Linguistic	Communicating ideas verbally and in writing; analyzing verbal and written communication	reader's theater, poetry, listening, retelling, choral speaking, creative writing, class discussions, dramatizing, writing diary entries
Logical-Mathematical	Problem-solving and classifying	predicting, surveys, measuring, classifying, scientific experiments, collecting data, solving puzzles
Bodily-Kinesthetic	Engaging in physical activities and hands-on activities	performing, crafts, computers, hands-on experiments, playing games
Visual-Spatial	Representing and arranging colors, shapes, and images; creating and interpreting graphs and charts	graphing, painting, illustrating information, designing posters, using charts, using graphic organizers, visualizing
Musical-Rhythmic	Creating and interpreting music and rhythmic patterns	humming, singing, writing poetry or songs, playing musical games, playing musical instruments, listening to music, rapping
Interpersonal	Working with groups and teams	cooperative learning, interviewing, group story writing, sharing, discussing, brainstorming, teaching others
Intrapersonal	Working independently	Independent projects, personal responses, independent reading, journals
Naturalist	Recognizing patterns in nature	observing animals and plants, collecting rocks and other natural objects, cleaning the environment, observing weather and the sky

Using the Books

Each book in the Steck-Vaughn *Multiple Intelligences* series includes 12 units, covering key topics in social studies and science. Each unit contains 9 activities, offering different approaches to instruction that appeal to a variety of intelligences and learning styles. Students learn about social studies or science not only through reading and writing, but they also learn by exploring their surroundings, participating in outdoor classrooms, performing, listening to and creating music, and working with their hands. In addition, each book contains a complete answer key.

Teachers and parents can use the activities in *Multiple Intelligences* to enhance, reinforce, and practice students' development in the core subjects of social studies and science. The activities may be used in any order.

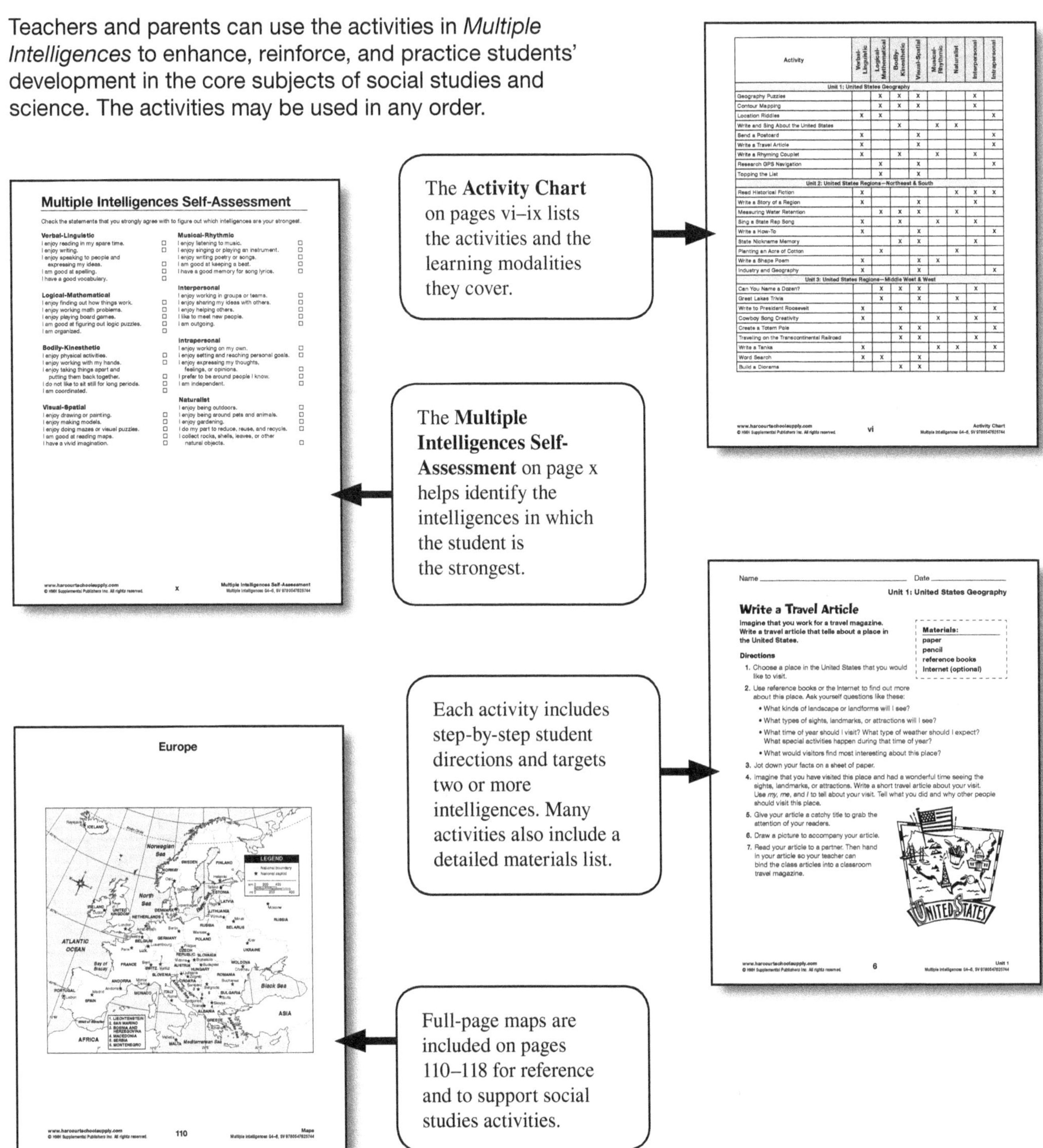

Activity	Verbal-Linguistic	Logical-Mathematical	Bodily-Kinesthetic	Visual-Spatial	Musical-Rhythmic	Naturalist	Interpersonal	Intrapersonal
Unit 1: United States Geography								
Geography Puzzles		X	X	X			X	
Contour Mapping		X	X	X			X	
Location Riddles	X	X						X
Write and Sing About the United States			X		X	X		
Send a Postcard	X			X				X
Write a Travel Article	X			X				X
Write a Rhyming Couplet	X		X		X		X	
Research GPS Navigation		X		X				X
Topping the List		X		X				
Unit 2: United States Regions—Northeast & South								
Read Historical Fiction	X					X	X	X
Write a Story of a Region	X			X			X	
Measuring Water Retention		X	X	X		X		
Sing a State Rap Song	X		X		X		X	
Write a How-To	X			X				X
State Nickname Memory			X	X			X	
Planting an Acre of Cotton		X				X		
Write a Shape Poem	X			X	X			
Industry and Geography	X			X				X
Unit 3: United States Regions—Middle West & West								
Can You Name a Dozen?		X	X	X			X	
Great Lakes Trivia		X		X		X		
Write to President Roosevelt	X		X					X
Cowboy Song Creativity	X				X		X	
Create a Totem Pole			X	X				X
Traveling on the Transcontinental Railroad			X	X			X	
Write a Tanka	X				X	X		X
Word Search	X	X		X				
Build a Diorama			X	X				

Multiple Intelligences G4–6, SV 9780547625744

Activity	Verbal-Linguistic	Logical-Mathematical	Bodily-Kinesthetic	Visual-Spatial	Musical-Rhythmic	Naturalist	Interpersonal	Intrapersonal
Unit 4: Land and Early People								
Reaching a Consensus	X						X	
Paint a Picture of a Poem				X	X	X		X
Create Native American Beads		X	X				X	
Play a Native American Game		X	X	X		X		
Write a Native American Tale	X			X				X
Make a Birchbark Canoe			X	X				
Imitate Inuit Throat-Singing	X		X		X		X	
Design a Lakota Winter Count	X	X		X				
Tell a Nature Story	X					X		
Unit 5: The American Revolution								
Give a Speech	X		X			X		X
Analyze a Political Cartoon		X		X			X	
Write a Descriptive Paragraph	X			X				X
Create a Silhouette Portrait	X		X	X				
Make Butter as You Sing			X		X		X	
Interpreting Graphs		X		X				X
Map Paul Revere's Ride		X			X		X	
Bake Colonial Brown Sugar Cookies		X	X				X	
Supporting Our Troops	X				X			X
Unit 6: Ancient Civilizations								
Create an Ancient Civilizations Mobile			X	X			X	
Build a Sumerian Ziggurat		X	X	X			X	
Compute Using Mayan Math		X	X	X		X		
Write Your Own Greek Myth	X							X
Make Natural Dye		X	X			X		
Research the Hanging Gardens of Babylon	X					X		X
Make an Egyptian Harp	X		X		X			
Athenian Acropolis	X			X			X	
Analyze Maps of Ancient Rome	X	X		X				X

Activity Chart
Multiple Intelligences G4–6, SV 9780547625744

Activity	Verbal-Linguistic	Logical-Mathematical	Bodily-Kinesthetic	Visual-Spatial	Musical-Rhythmic	Naturalist	Interpersonal	Intrapersonal
Unit 7: Australia and the South Pacific								
Be an Expert		X	X	X			X	
Acrostic Animals	X			X				X
Make a Didgeridoo			X	X	X			
Sing "Waltzing Matilda"			X		X	X	X	
A Talking Statue	X							X
South Pacific Dream Island Vacation	X	X		X			X	
Create a Sidewalk Mural of Australia			X	X			X	
Hooping the Islands		X	X	X		X		
A Trip to New Zealand	X	X						X
Unit 8: Europe								
Name That Country	X	X		X		X	X	
Sing a European Song	X				X		X	
Make Tzatziki		X	X	X				
Design a Board Game	X		X	X			X	
Plan a Menu	X	X						X
Famous Places Bingo			X	X				
Play German Games			X			X		
Write a Pen Pal Letter	X							X
Make a Picture Dictionary	X			X				X
Unit 9: Asia								
Analyze a Cartogram		X		X				X
Write a Haiku	X				X	X		X
Make Date Macaroons		X	X	X			X	
What Animal Are You?	X	X		X				
Write a Chant	X		X		X	X		
Make a Historical Map		X	X	X			X	
Research an Asian Culture	X	X		X				X
Outdoor Reader's Theater	X		X			X	X	
Draw a Manga Comic Strip		X		X				

Activity Chart
Multiple Intelligences G4–6, SV 9780547625744

Activity	Verbal-Linguistic	Logical-Mathematical	Bodily-Kinesthetic	Visual-Spatial	Musical-Rhythmic	Naturalist	Interpersonal	Intrapersonal
Unit 10: Africa								
Build an African Zoo	X		X	X				X
Play a Logic Game	X	X		X				
Write an African Tale	X							X
Write an African Praise Song	X		X		X		X	
Create a Mask for the Festival of Masks		X		X	X	X	X	
Construct a Pyramid Bedroom		X	X	X				X
Play Mamba			X			X		
Make and Play a Mancala Game		X	X			X	X	
Weather in Africa	X	X	X	X			X	
Unit 11: North America								
Working at a Maquiladora			X	X			X	
Charting Longitude and Latitude		X		X			X	
Sail on an Alaskan Cruise	X	X				X		X
Write a Capital Song	X			X	X			
Design a Viking Ship	X	X		X				
Central American Dances			X		X		X	
Measure the Pan-American Highway		X		X				X
Make Guacamole	X	X	X					
A Man, a Plan, a Canal: Panama	X	X				X		X
Unit 12: South America								
Make a Pie Chart		X		X			X	
Perform a Song	X		X		X			
Create a Pottery Design		X		X				X
Catalog Plants and Animals			X	X		X		
Draw a Diagram of the Catatumbo Lightning		X		X		X		
Design Paper People			X	X				X
Create a South American Travel Brochure	X					X		
Make a Travel Invitation	X			X			X	
Perform a South American Chant	X		X		X			

Activity Chart
Multiple Intelligences G4–6, SV 9780547625744

Multiple Intelligences Self-Assessment

Check the statements that you strongly agree with to figure out which intelligences are your strongest.

Verbal-Linguistic

I enjoy reading in my spare time. ☐
I enjoy writing. ☐
I enjoy speaking to people and
   expressing my ideas. ☐
I am good at spelling. ☐
I have a good vocabulary. ☐

Logical-Mathematical

I enjoy finding out how things work. ☐
I enjoy working math problems. ☐
I enjoy playing board games. ☐
I am good at figuring out logic puzzles. ☐
I am organized. ☐

Bodily-Kinesthetic

I enjoy physical activities. ☐
I enjoy working with my hands. ☐
I enjoy taking things apart and
   putting them back together. ☐
I do not like to sit still for long periods. ☐
I am coordinated. ☐

Visual-Spatial

I enjoy drawing or painting. ☐
I enjoy making models. ☐
I enjoy doing mazes or visual puzzles. ☐
I am good at reading maps. ☐
I have a vivid imagination. ☐

Musical-Rhythmic

I enjoy listening to music. ☐
I enjoy singing or playing an instrument. ☐
I enjoy writing poetry or songs. ☐
I am good at keeping a beat. ☐
I have a good memory for song lyrics. ☐

Interpersonal

I enjoy working in groups or teams. ☐
I enjoy sharing my ideas with others. ☐
I enjoy helping others. ☐
I like to meet new people. ☐
I am outgoing. ☐

Intrapersonal

I enjoy working on my own. ☐
I enjoy setting and reaching personal goals. ☐
I enjoy expressing my thoughts,
   feelings, or opinions. ☐
I prefer to be around people I know. ☐
I am independent. ☐

Naturalist

I enjoy being outdoors. ☐
I enjoy being around pets and animals. ☐
I enjoy gardening. ☐
I do my part to reduce, reuse, and recycle. ☐
I collect rocks, shells, leaves, or other
   natural objects. ☐

Multiple Intelligences Self-Assessment
Multiple Intelligences G4–6, SV 9780547625744

Geography Puzzles

Each of the fifty states has a unique shape. Can you look at a geography puzzle and identify the states?

Directions

1. Work with a group to cut apart several large sections of a blank United States map.

2. Give each member a section of the map. Cut apart the states in your section. (Some of the smaller states in the northeast can be grouped together.)

3. Shuffle all of the states and spread them out on the table. As a group, put together several states to make a picture.

4. Glue the states to one side of a sheet of construction paper. On the back, list the states used to make the geography puzzle. See the geography puzzle of a firefighter below for an example. (Your puzzle will not include the state abbreviations.)

5. Trade puzzles with another group. Try to identify as many states as possible without looking at a U.S. map. List the states on a separate sheet of paper. Look at the back of the puzzle to check your answers.

6. Trade puzzles again and keep playing until your group has solved every puzzle.

Materials:

construction paper

paper

pencil

scissors

glue stick

U.S. map

blank U.S. map

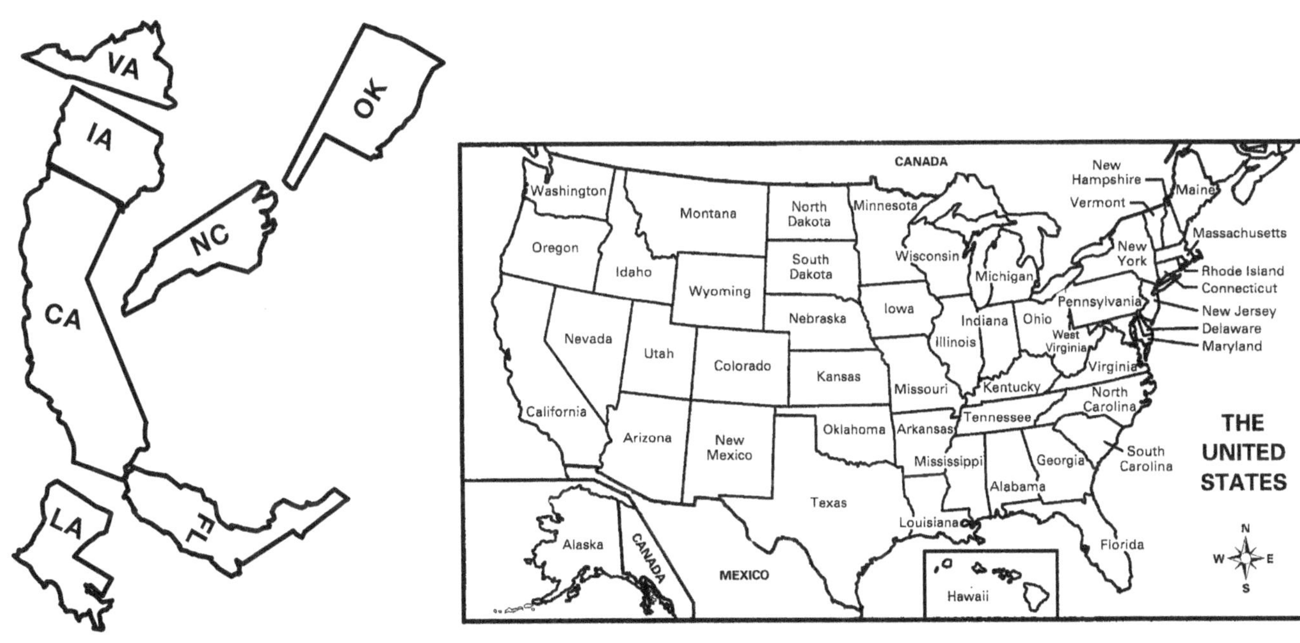

Contour Mapping

Maps are flat, but land is not. Land is made up of many landforms. A landform is a feature that makes up Earth's surface, such as mountains, valleys, cliffs, and plains.

Contour maps show the height of land. These maps use contour lines. Contour lines form closed circles around the tops of hills, mountains, and valleys. They connect places of the same height. Closely spaced contour lines represent a steep slope. Widely spaced contour lines represent a gentle slope.

Directions

1. As a group, study the contour map of Hawaii. Discuss these questions:

   - What kind of landform is shown in the contour map? How do you know?

   - Where are the contour lines spaced close together?

   - Where are they spaced wide apart?

2. Draw an outline of Hawaii's contour map on a piece of cardboard.

3. Work together to fill in the outline with clay.

4. Use more clay to build up the surface. Use the contour lines as a guide.

5. Use a pencil to carve the contour lines.

6. Walk around the room and look at the other contour maps. They should look about the same as yours.

7. Discuss any differences you noticed and why those differences occurred among the maps.

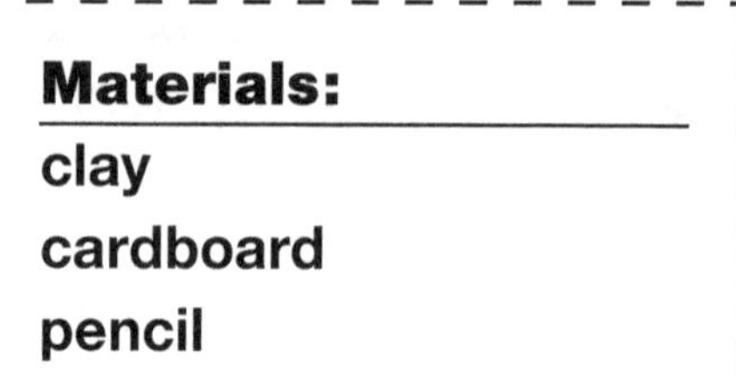

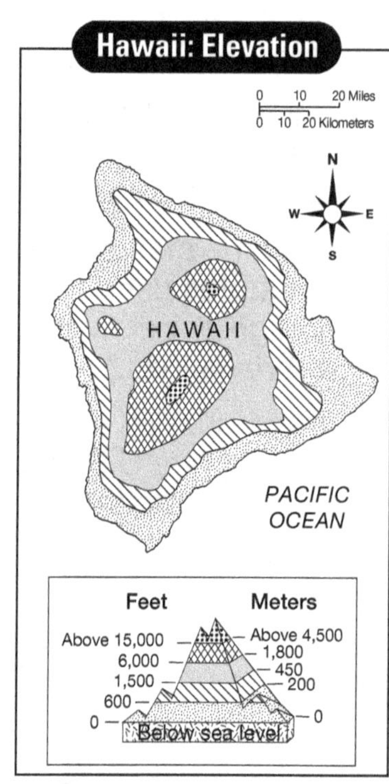

Contour Map of Hawaii

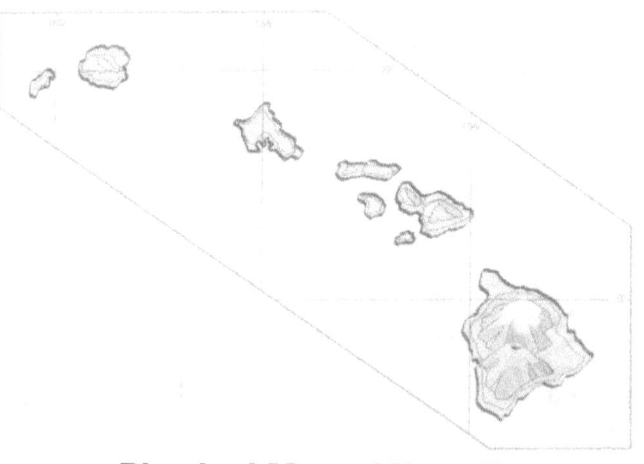

Physical Map of Hawaii

Location Riddles

Maps and globes can be divided into smaller sections by a series of lines called longitude and latitude. Lines of longitude pass through the North Pole and South Pole. Lines of latitude circle the globe. The equator is the longest line of latitude. Use lines of longitude and latitude to write a riddle about a place in the United States. Can your classmates guess the answer?

Materials:

index card

pencil

map of the United States (showing longitude and latitude)

Directions

1. Choose any place in the United States. Use a map of the United States to help you find the specific location.

2. Write a riddle with clues on an index card. Include lines of longitude and/or latitude. Write the answer underneath your riddle. See the example below.

3. Read your riddle aloud. Let others use a map or globe to guess the answer.

4. Let classmates guess until someone answers correctly.

5. Now try to answer other class riddles!

I am a city in the western United States.
My line of longitude is about 120° W.
I am northeast of Salem.
I begin with the letter *P*.
What city am I?
(Answer: Portland, Oregon)

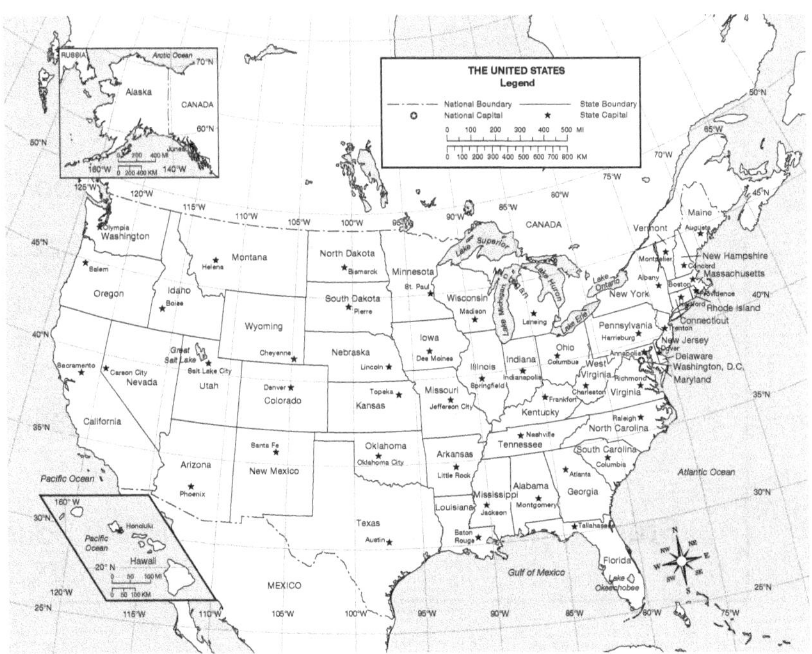

Write and Sing About the United States

Many songs have been written about the United States. Choose your favorite from the list below. Then write another verse for that song and sing it to the class.

Directions

<table>
<tr><td valign="top">

1. Work with a group and choose a song from the list below. Use reference books or the Internet to find the song lyrics for the chosen song. Copy or print the song lyrics.

</td><td valign="top">

Materials:
paper
pencil
outdoor spot
print out of song lyrics
reference books
Internet (optional)

</td></tr>
</table>

2. Find an outdoor spot and sit with your group. Read over the lyrics of the song your group has chosen. Sing the chorus and one or two verses of the song. Clap out the rhythm as you sing the song.

3. Work with your group to write another verse to the song. Discuss these questions:

   - What is the song's message about the United States?

   - How does the song express patriotism?

   - What kinds of landforms or places are mentioned in the song?

   - How do these landforms or places compare to one another?

4. After all groups have finished, sit in a large circle. Take turns performing your song and discussing the answers to the questions.

Songs About the United States

God Bless the U.S.A. - Lee Greenwood

This Land Is Your Land - Woody Guthrie

My Country 'Tis of Thee - Samuel Francis Smith

Back in the U.S.A. - Chuck Berry

America the Beautiful - Katharine Lee Bates

God Bless America - Irving Berlin

Stars and Stripes Forever - John Phillip Sousa

Send a Postcard

It's fun to send postcards from places we visit. It's fun to receive them, too! Choose a state and make a postcard to give to a classmate.

Materials:
index card
pencil
crayons

Directions

1. Choose a well-known place in the United States, such as the Washington Monument, Statue of Liberty, Yellowstone National Park, or the Grand Canyon.

2. On the blank side of an index card, draw the outline of the state where the well-known place is located. Mark the location and draw a picture of the well-known place and include a brief description.

3. On the back of the postcard, write a paragraph about the state that includes the following information:

   - the capital city of the state

   - other places of interest and a few landforms in the state

   - names of bordering states

4. Exchange postcards with a classmate. Study the picture and read the back of the postcard.

5. Return the postcard and tell your classmate one thing you learned about that state.

Write a Travel Article

Imagine that you work for a travel magazine. Write a travel article that tells about a place in the United States.

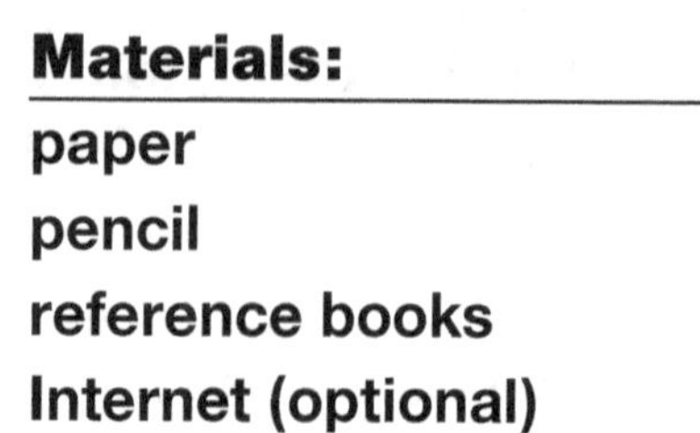

Directions

1. Choose a place in the United States that you would like to visit.

2. Use reference books or the Internet to find out more about this place. Ask yourself questions like these:

   - What kinds of landscape or landforms will I see?

   - What types of sights, landmarks, or attractions will I see?

   - What time of year should I visit? What type of weather should I expect? What special activities happen during that time of year?

   - What would visitors find most interesting about this place?

3. Jot down your facts on a sheet of paper.

4. Imagine that you have visited this place and had a wonderful time seeing the sights, landmarks, or attractions. Write a short travel article about your visit. Use *my*, *me*, and *I* to tell about your visit. Tell what you did and why other people should visit this place.

5. Give your article a catchy title to grab the attention of your readers.

6. Draw a picture to accompany your article.

7. Read your article to a partner. Then hand in your article so your teacher can bind the class articles into a classroom travel magazine.

Name _________________________________   Date _______________

Write a Rhyming Couplet

A couplet is two lines of poetry that usually rhyme. Write a rhyming couplet that tells about a region of the United States.

Materials:

paper
pencil

Directions

1. Close your eyes and picture the scenery in different parts of the United States.

2. Choose one place and write a couplet about what you see in your mind.

3. Join other classmates to form a small group.

4. Read your couplet to the group. Listen while others read their couplets.

5. String the couplets together to make a longer poem.

6. Read the poem together and clap out the beat. Rehearse the poem until your entire group sounds fluent.

7. Perform your couplet poem for the class. Vary the pitch and tone of your voice to make the reading more dramatic.

**The lighthouse soldier at his post
guards New England's rocky coast.**

Research GPS Navigation

Today maps are often produced by computers, using satellite images taken from space. The Global Positioning System (GPS) is a satellite navigation system. Many cars and cell phones are equipped with GPS navigation systems. As cities change and new roads are built, GPS navigation systems can show us the updated information and help us find our way.

Materials:
paper
poster board
pencil
markers
reference books
Internet (optional)

Directions

1. Use reference books or the Internet to find out how GPS satellite navigation works. Write down questions you have like the ones below:

   - When was GPS first used and by whom?

   - How many satellites are used and where are they located?

   - How do GPS receivers obtain information from the satellites?

2. Conduct research to find out the answers to your questions. Take notes.

3. Use your notes to create a diagram on a sheet of poster board.

4. Label your diagram and write captions to explain how GPS navigation works.

5. Present your poster to the class and then display it in the classroom for future reference.

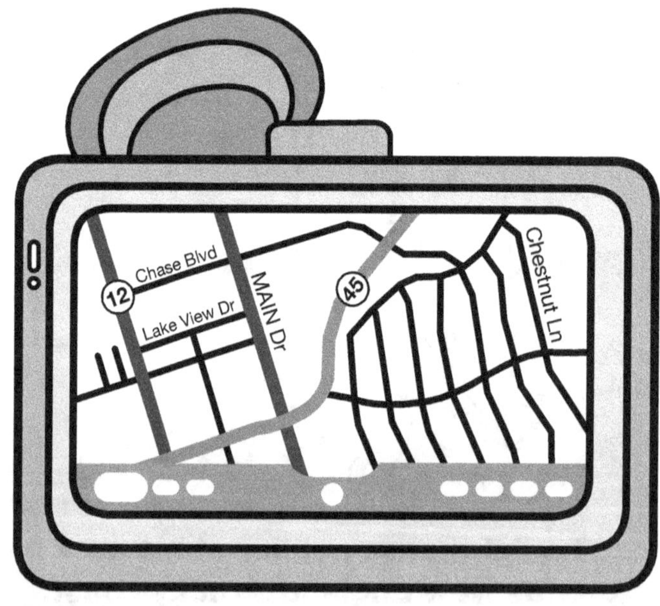

Topping the List

The Empire State Building is a famous landmark in New York City. When the building opened in 1931, it was the tallest building in the world. The Empire State Building has been named one of the Seven Wonders of the Modern World by the American Society of Civil Engineers. It is over 1,000 feet tall. Currently, the Empire State Building is the third tallest building in the United States. What other buildings are in the top three list?

Materials:

paper
reference books
Internet (optional)
pencil
ruler

Directions

1. Work with a group to research the top three tallest buildings in the United States. Use reference books or the Internet to find out the answers to the questions below:

   - What are the names of the three tallest buildings in the United States?

   - Where is each located?

   - When was each completed?

   - How tall is each building? (Do not include antenna masts.)

   - How many floors does each building have?

2. Use the data you have gathered to create a bar graph that compares the height of the three tallest buildings in the United States.

3. Below the bar graph, write a paragraph about each of the buildings that includes the answers to the questions above.

9

Read Historical Fiction

Historical fiction tells a story that is set in the past. Many historical fiction novels take place in specific regions of the United States, such as the Northeast and the South. Read a historical fiction novel to learn more about one of these regions.

Materials:

outdoor spot

historical fiction novel

journal or spiral notebook

Directions

1. With a partner or a small literature group, choose a historical fiction novel that takes place in the Northeast or the South. Some suggestions are listed below.

2. Sit together outside. Discuss the title, author, and the names of the chapters. Look at the cover of the book and any pictures inside.

3. Take turns reading the first few chapters. Pause and discuss what has happened so far. After the discussion, reflect on the book and write down what you've learned about the characters and the setting.

4. Meet periodically to read together. After each session, each member writes down one question for discussion. Continue in this manner until you have finished reading the book.

The South

Graveyard Girl; by Anna Myers; © 1995; Walker Publishing; (Memphis during the 1878 yellow fever epidemic)

Shades of Gray; by Carolyn Reeder; © 1999; Perfection Learning; (post-Civil War Virginia)

The Watsons go to Birmingham—1963; by Christopher Paul Curtis; ©1995; Delecorte Books for Young Readers (Civil Rights movement in Alabama)

V for Victor; by Mark Childress; © 1998; Ballantine Books; (Alabama during WW II)

The Northeast

Johnny Tremain; by Esther Forbes; © 1943; Houghton Mifflin; (Boston during the outbreak of the American Revolution)

The Courage of Sarah Noble; by Alice Dalgliesh; © 1954; Scribner; (northeast during colonization)

The Night the Bells Rang; by Natalie Kinsey-Warnock; © 1991; Puffin (Vermont during last year of WW I)

The Sign of the Beaver; by Elizabeth George Speare; © 1983; Houghton Mifflin (Maine during the colonial era)

Unit 2: United States Regions—Northeast & South

Write a Story of a Region

Geography affects people, places, and environments. Create a picture book for young children that tells about the geography of a state in the Northeast. (Connecticut, Maine, Massachusetts, New Hampshire, Rhode Island, Vermont, New Jersey, New York, or Pennsylvania.)

Materials:

- pencil
- crayons or colored pencils
- blank sheets of paper
- reference books
- Internet (optional)
- stapler

Directions

1. Choose a state in the Northeast. Use reference books or the Internet to conduct research to find out about its:

   types of resources   weather and climate   major cities

   landforms and bodies of water   famous landmarks

2. Jot down your notes on a sheet of paper. Choose the most interesting facts to include in your picture book. Remember that your book will be read to younger children.

3. Write a few sentences about your state on each sheet of blank paper. Illustrate each page.

4. Make a cover for your book and write the title on the front cover.

5. Staple the pages together and read your book aloud to a group of younger children.

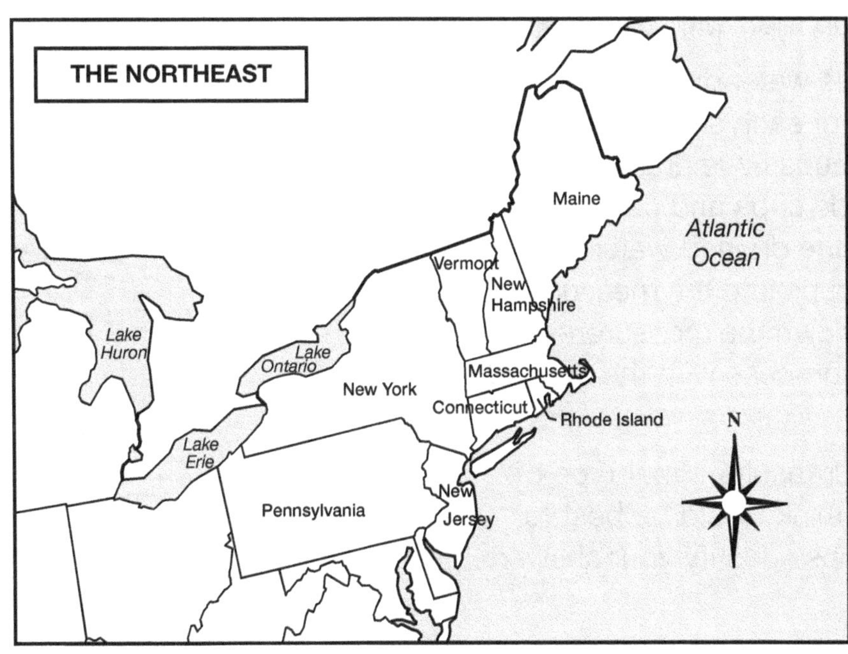

Multiple Intelligences G4–6, SV 9780547625744

Unit 2: United States Regions—Northeast & South

Measuring Water Retention

Water retention is the amount of water that soil can hold. If soil retains too much water, plants receive too much water and die. If soil does not retain water, plants receive too little water and die. Different regions of the country have different types of soil that support a variety of crops. The rich soil in Southern states, like Georgia, North Carolina, and Virginia, is well-suited for growing crops. On the other hand, the rocky soil in Maine and Vermont makes farming a bit more challenging. Conduct an experiment to find out why.

Materials:

paper towel tube
2 small Styrofoam cups
2 large Styrofoam cups
measuring cup
scissors
pencil
paper
pebbles
potting soil

Directions

1. Work with a group to complete this experiment. Take the two small Styrofoam cups and gently push the sharp end of a pencil through the bottom of each to make a small drainage hole.

2. Fill one small cup completely with soil. Fill three-quarters of the other small cup with pebbles and then top with a thin layer of soil.

3. Cut two 3-inch rings from a cardboard paper towel tube. Place the rings in the bottom of the two larger, empty Styrofoam cups. Set the soil- and pebble-filled cups inside of the larger cups, so that they rest on the top of the cardboard ring.

4. Slowly pour ½ cup of water into the small cup filled with soil. Repeat the process for the small cup filled with pebbles.

5. Watch as the water drains through the bottom of each small cup. When both small cups have drained, take out the inside cups and cardboard rings. Pour the drained water from one of the cups into the measuring cup. Write down the measurement. Repeat the process with the second cup.

6. Discuss your results. What type of soil do you think would be best for growing crops? Justify your answers.

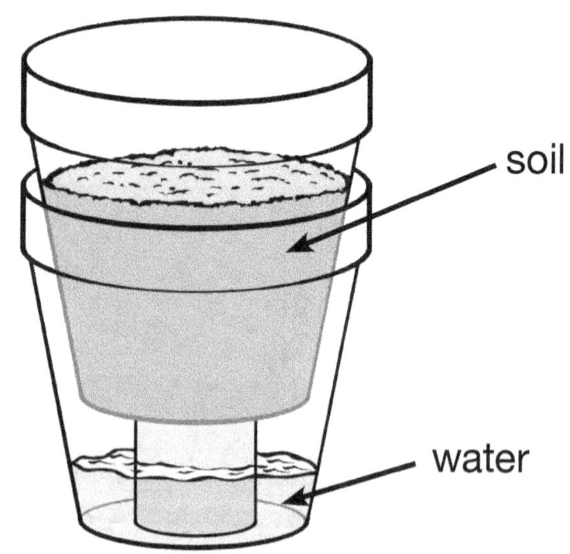

Unit 2: United States Regions—Northeast & South

Sing a State Rap Song

Can you and your classmates write a rap song to help you remember the names of the northeastern and southern states?

Directions

1. Each member makes two lists using the maps below. One list names the northeastern states. The other list names the southern states. Study both lists for 15-20 seconds.

2. On a second sheet of paper, try to duplicate the two lists from memory. Write down as many states from each region as you can remember. How many did you remember?

3. As a group, write a rap song. Your rap may or may not rhyme. Include the names of all southern and northeastern states. Make sure your song teaches which ones are which.

4. Practice singing your rap song. Clap to the rhythm.

5. Perform your rap song for others.

6. Afterwards, try to duplicate the two lists of states again from memory. Write down as many states from each region as you can remember. How many did you remember this time? How well did the rap song improve your memory? Discuss how music can help memorization.

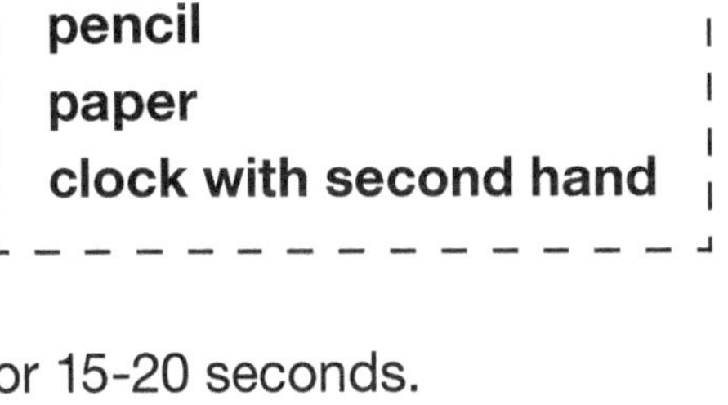

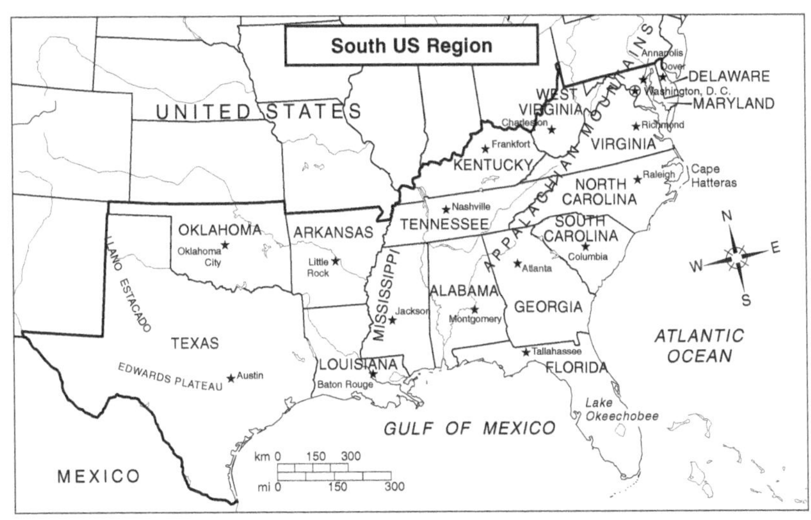

Unit 2: United States Regions—Northeast & South

Write a How-To

Logging is an important industry in Maine, New Hampshire, and Vermont. Use the picture below to write about how paper is produced from trees.

Directions

1. Study the diagram below. It shows how logs are used to produce paper. Use the diagram and reference books or the Internet to help you explain the step-by-step process.

2. Use transition words such as *first*, *next*, *then*, and *finally* to help you order the steps.

3. When you are finished, read your paper to a partner. Then, listen as your partner reads his or her paper to you. Compare both papers. Did both of you include every step?

> **Materials:**
> paper
> pencil
> reference books
> Internet (optional)

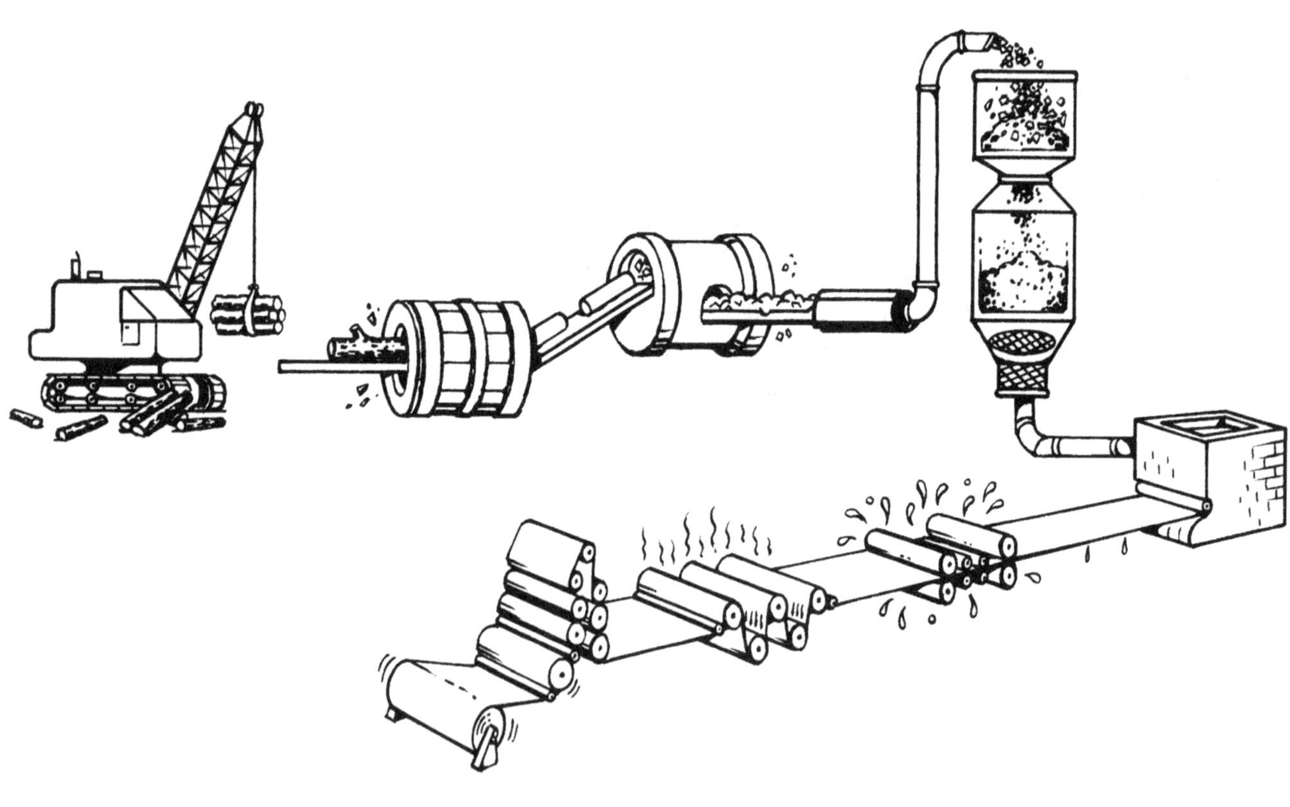

Unit 2: United States Regions—Northeast & South

State Nickname Memory

How well do you know your state nicknames? Play memory to find out.

Virginia	Georgia	Maryland
Maine	New York	Vermont
Florida	Kentucky	Tennessee
Delaware	Rhode Island	Massachussetts

Materials:

almanac or reference
  books
Internet (optional)
24 index cards
pencils

Directions

1. Form groups of four. Each group member will have six index cards.

   a) Choose three states listed in the box and write the names on the front of index cards. Each state should be written down only once.

   b) Use the Internet or other reference books to find out the nickname for each of your three states.

   c) Write the nickname of each state on the front of the three remaining index cards.

2. As a group, spend 2-3 minutes reading all of the state nicknames.

3. Set all the index cards writing side down in four rows of six on a table. Each group member will take turns flipping over two cards. If the two cards match the state name with the state nickname, the player removes the two cards from the rows and plays another turn.

4. If the two cards do not match the state name and state nickname, the player turns the cards back over, and the next player goes. Players should pay attention to where the cards are located to improve their chances of matching.

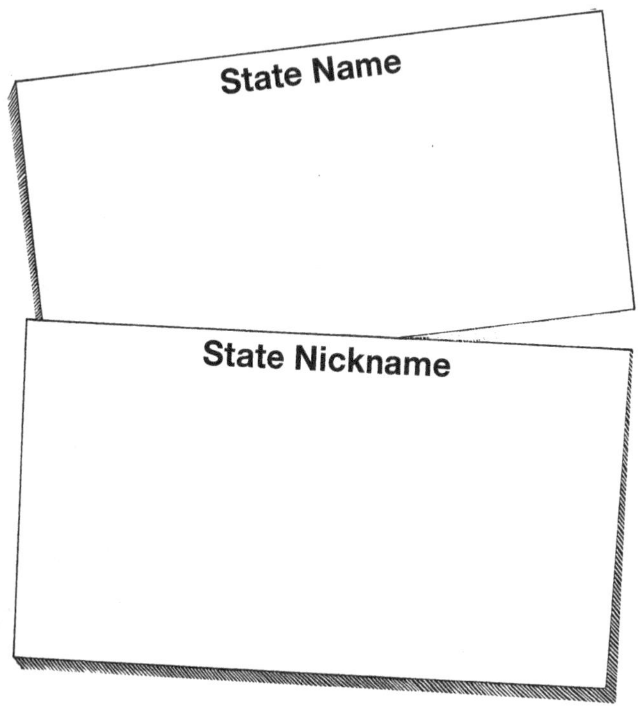

Multiple Intelligences G4–6, SV 9780547625744

Planting an Acre of Cotton

Many of our nation's crops are grown in the South. Long ago in the southern colonies, cotton was an important cash crop. A cash crop is a plentiful crop that is easy to raise and sell for money. Suppose you lived during in the South during the colonial era. How much cotton would you be able to grow on a square acre of land?

Materials: ___________

paper

pencil

Directions

Use the information below to answer questions 1–4. Then, on a separate sheet of paper draw a diagram of two rows with planting instructions.

- A square acre is about 209 feet in length.
- Cotton plants should be spaced 4 inches apart.
- Rows of cotton should be 40 inches apart.

1. About how many feet wide is a square acre? ___________

2. About how many rows of cotton would you be able to plant in a square acre? ___________

3. About how many cotton plants would fit in each row? ___________

4. About how many cotton plants would you have altogether? ___________

Unit 2: United States Regions—Northeast & South

Write a Shape Poem

A shape poem is a poem in which all of the lines are written inside of a shape. A shape poem about Texas, for example, would look like the shape of Texas. Write and chant a shape poem about a state in the South or Northeast.

Directions

1. Choose any state in the South or Northeast. Use reference books or the Internet to locate interesting facts about the state. Write down the facts on an index card so you will have them handy.

2. Draw an outline of the state you chose on a sheet of drawing paper. Use a United States map to help you draw the shape.

3. Use the facts on your index card to help you write a shape poem about your chosen state.

4. Practice reading or chanting your poem aloud. Pay attention to the rhythm of the lines and revise your wording if necessary to improve the rhythm. Then, perform your poem for the class. Display your shape poem in the classroom.

Materials:

drawing paper
index card
pencil
reference books
Internet (optional)
U.S. map

Multiple Intelligences G4–6, SV 9780547625744

Unit 2: United States Regions—Northeast & South

Industry and Geography

How does geography affect the products and resources of a region? Study the map below to find out.

Directions

Use the map below to answer the following quesitons.

1. What resources and products are most common in the South?

____

2. What resources and products are most common in the Northeast?

____

3. Based on the map, how do you think the geography of a state affects the kinds of jobs people hold?

____

Multiple Intelligences G4–6, SV 9780547625744

Unit 3: United States Regions—Middle West & West

Can You Name a Dozen?

There are a dozen states that make up the Middle West. Can you name them all?

Directions

1. Use a United States map to help you label the 12 states that make up the Middle West region. Write their names on the map below.

2. Cut the states apart and shuffle them face-up on a table or desk.

3. Without looking at the U.S. map, race against a partner to see who can correctly put the states together again.

4. Then take turns asking questions such as, "Which state borders Canada and Minnesota?" (North Dakota). Use your map to help you.

Materials:

pencil

scissors

U.S. map

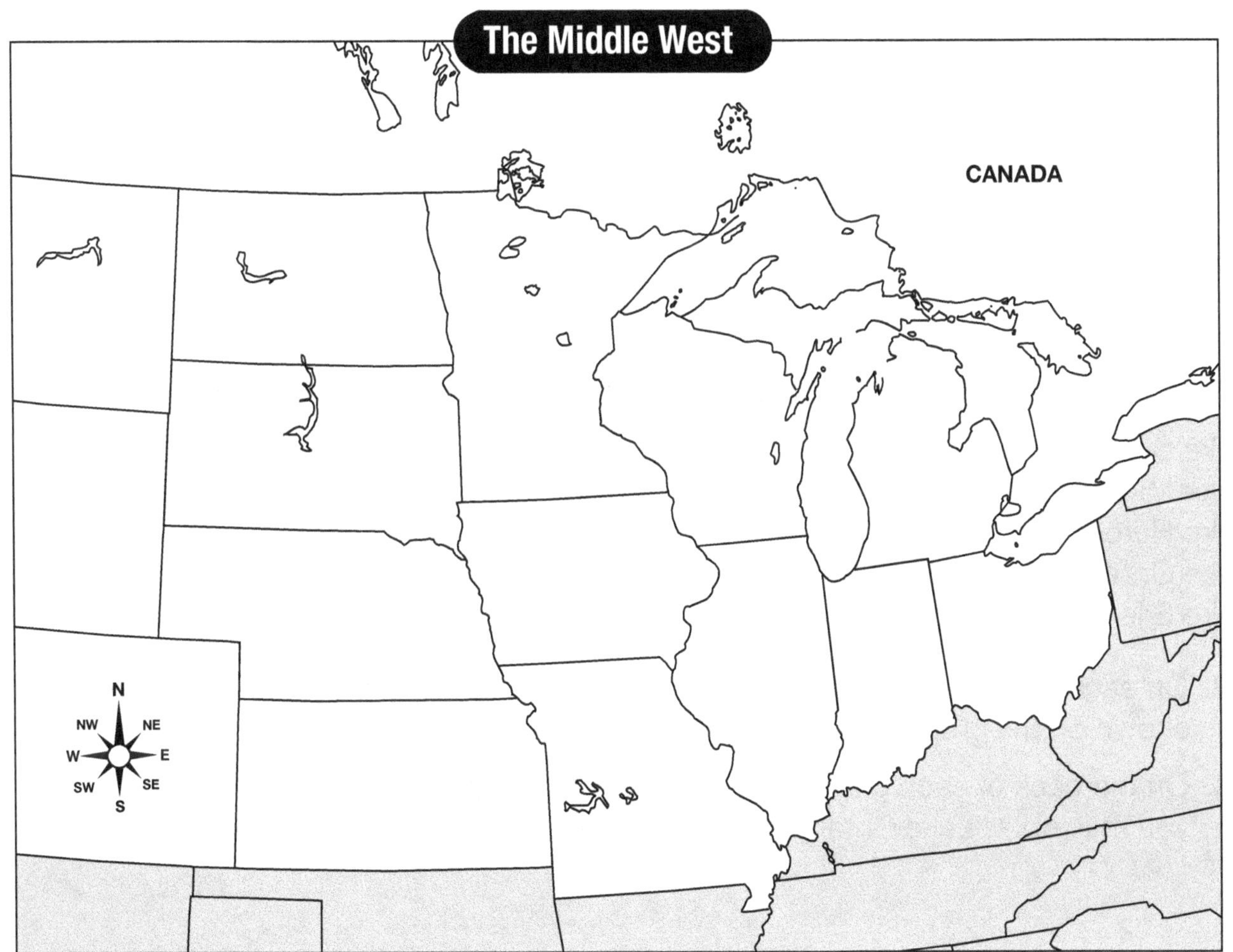

Unit 3: United States Regions—Middle West & West

Great Lakes Trivia

How much do you know about the Great Lakes? Take some time to learn more about each of these lakes and create a series of bar graphs to display what you've learned.

Directions

1. Use the information and map below to make a series of bar graphs about the Great Lakes.

   Each year, a small amount of water flows out of the Great Lakes. Each of the Great Lakes has a different lake retention time. Lake retention time is the calculated amount of time it would take for all of the water in a lake to drain as new water replaces it.

Maximum Depths of the Great Lakes

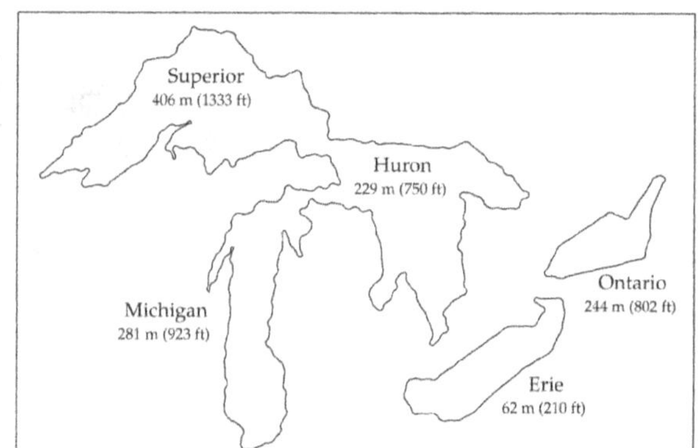

Lakes Retention Time of the Great Lakes

Lake Superior	191 years
Lake Michigan	99 years
Lake Huron	22 years
Lake Ontario	6 years
Lake Erie	2.6 years

Average Depth of the Great Lakes

Lake Superior	483 feet
Lake Michigan	279 feet
Lake Huron	195 feet
Lake Ontario	283 feet
Lake Erie	62 feet

Surface Area of the Great Lakes

Lake Superior	31,700 square miles
Lake Michigan	22,300 square miles
Lake Huron	23,000 square miles
Lake Ontario	7,340 square miles
Lake Erie	9,910 square miles

2. On each graph, include the title, labels, and the scale, or the unit of measure shown on the graph. Color the bars to make them stand out.

3. On the back of each graph, write a paragraph comparing the data. (For example, you may note "Lake Ontario drains three times faster than Lake Huron.")

Unit 3: United States Regions—Middle West & West

Write to President Roosevelt

During the 1930s, a large part of the Great Plains became known as the **Dust Bowl.** Severe drought caused dry soil. As the wind whipped through the plains, it picked up the dry topsoil and created terrible dust storms that lasted for years. Imagine that your family is living in the Great Plains during the 1930s. Write a letter to President Franklin Delano Roosevelt asking for help.

The Dust Bowl

The Dust Bowl of the 1930s caused devastation for almost ten years. The drought and dust caused cattle and crops to die. People and animals had nothing to eat. Huge dust storms called black blizzards darkened the sky and blew dust 2,000 miles away. People breathed in dust and had many health problems. Dust filled their lungs and stomachs. It covered their bodies. Many people died and animals died. People were trapped in their homes. Dust blew through cracks in windows and under doors. It filled houses. Without jobs, food, money, or proper healthcare, people needed massive amounts of help. Many farmers lost their farms. Some families stayed, while others moved away. President Franklin Delano Roosevelt and his administration organized a huge drought relief program. The government spent $1 billion dollars to help families recover from the drought.

Directions

1. Reflect on the information presented in the paragraph above. Imagine that you and your family are farmers living in the Great Plains region in the 1930s. You have heard that the government wants to provide relief.

2. On a separate sheet of paper, write a letter to President Franklin Delano Roosevelt asking for his help. Tell him what state you live in, how your family has suffered, what your day-to-day life is like, and how you feel. Be specific.

3. Fold your letter and put it in an envelope. Address your letter and trade envelopes with a partner.

4. Read your parent's letter and discuss how the letters are similar or different.

Unit 3: United States Regions—Middle West & West

Cowboy Song Creativity

"Home on the Range" is a traditional cowboy song that describes the West. Sing it with your classmates and let it inspire your own creativity.

Materials:

paper
pencil
colored pencils

Home on the Range

Oh give me a home where the buffalo roam,
Where the deer and the antelope play;
Where never is heard a discouraging word
And the skies are not cloudy all day.

Chorus: Home, home on the range,
Where the deer and the antelope play;
Where never is heard a discouraging word
And the skies are not cloudy all day.

How often at night, when the heavens are bright,
With the light from the glittering stars,
Have I stood there amazed, and asked as I gazed
If their glory exceeds that of ours.

Chorus: Home, home on the range,
Where the deer and the antelope play;
Where never is heard a discouraging word
And the skies are not cloudy all day.

Directions

1. Reflect on the words of the song. Imagine what it would be like to stand in an open field on the range during the day and then at night. Consider the following:

   - How would the scene look different during the day and during the night?

   - How would you feel during the different times of the day?

2. Draw and color a picture to show the two scenes.

3. Write a few sentences under each picture to describe the scene and how it makes you feel.

Create a Totem Pole

A totem pole is a post carved from a large tree.
Totem poles display a series of painted faces.
Each face is a symbol that represents a family or
clan. Totem poles are carved by Native American
peoples who live along the Pacific Northwest Coast.
(Oregon, Washington, and Alaska) Make a totem
pole that represents your family or another group.

> **Materials:**
> paper towel tube
> drawing paper
> markers or colored
>   pencils
> scissors
> tape

Directions

1. Wrap a piece of drawing paper around a cardboard
   paper towel tube so that the entire tube is covered.

2. Cut off the overlapping paper in the back.

3. Decide what group you would like the totem pole to represent.
   It could represent your family, school, classroom, circle of friends,
   or community. Once you decide, think about symbols that represent
   character traits of the group.

4. Draw and color different faces or
   symbols to represent members of
   your chosen group.

5. Wrap the drawing paper around the
   tube and tape the seam in the back.
   Extend tape into the ends of the tube
   so that the paper does not slide off.

6. Display your tube and explain the
   meaning behind the symbols and
   faces.

Multiple Intelligences G4–6, SV 9780547625744

Unit 3: United States Regions—Middle West & West

Traveling on the Transcontinental Railroad

The Transcontinental Railroad was built between 1863 and 1869 and passed through five states in the Middle West and West. The Transcontinental Railroad linked with the existing railroad in the East, and together they formed the first railroad that stretched from the Atlantic to the Pacific. Travel on the Transcontinental Railroad with your group.

Materials:

5 index cards

scissors

tape

construction paper

reference books

Internet (optional)

Directions

1. Work in a group of five. Each member will research one of the five states through which the Transcontinental Railroad passed.

2. Using reference books or the Internet, each member finds the answers to the questions below about the chosen state:

   • Which railroad company laid the tracks in the state?

   • Which cities did the railroad pass through?

   • What landforms does the railroad cover?

3. Write the answers on the lined side of the index card.

4. On the blank side of the index card, write the name of the state. Then draw a picture of the landforms and scenery one might see through the window of the train.

5. Have one member draw and cut the train engine and wheels from a sheet of construction paper.

6. Order the index cards so that the westernmost state is first and the easternmost state is last. Then, tape the scenery side of the westernmost state to the engine to create the first train car. Add the remaining index cards to complete the train.

7. Tape the wheels on the train and stand the train accordion fashion and view the different landscapes.

8. Take turns reading facts about each state.

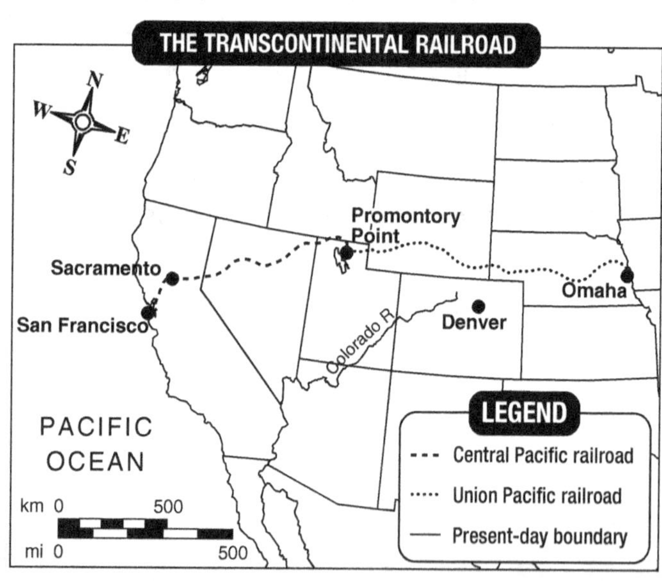

Write a Tanka

A tanka is a Japanese poem that follows a certain pattern. It has five unrhymed lines of five, seven, five, seven, and seven syllables. Write a tanka about the West.

Materials:
paper
pencil
drawing paper
a quiet outdoor spot

Directions

1. Find a quiet spot outside. Read the tanka below and clap out the 5-7-5-7-7 pattern.

2. Close your eyes and picture the West. What does it look like? What sounds do you hear?

3. Use your ideas to write a tanka. Clap and count until you have formed a 5-7-5-7-7 pattern. See the example below.

4. Illustrate your poem on a sheet of drawing paper. Find a partner and share your tanka.

Out West

Huge mesas and cliffs
and big prickly cactuses
decorate the West,
a vast and peaceful region
where I can rest and relax.

Unit 3: United States Regions—Middle West & West

Word Search

Complete the word search and see if you can find 12 different places in 12 different Middle West and West states.

Directions

1. Circle the name of the 12 places. Answers may be forward, backward, horizontal, vertical, or diagonal.

2. As you find each place in the puzzle, write the state abbreviation in the blank beside the corresponding place. Use a United States map if you need help.

```
S  M  S  R  M  W  N  R  O  U  R  R  I  F  G
E  Q  A  R  B  H  O  O  D  R  I  V  E  R  O
N  M  N  O  Y  N  A  C  D  N  A  R  G  E  Q
I  R  T  T  W  J  O  H  S  L  O  S  L  I  T
O  G  A  C  I  H  C  H  J  M  A  P  D  S  R
M  X  F  C  Q  N  K  O  H  L  L  T  D  G  T
S  N  E  L  E  H  T  S  T  N  U  O  M  X  J
E  K  N  A  X  I  U  L  M  Q  O  C  W  O  G
D  S  W  H  C  R  A  Y  A  W  E  T  A  G  I
A  N  S  I  T  K  A  Y  R  V  P  G  W  W  D
R  E  V  N  E  D  V  I  P  H  F  T  Q  E  Z
Q  T  U  C  R  E  U  G  O  N  W  L  G  U  I
P  O  I  P  S  M  B  C  F  Z  J  F  B  D  W
M  T  D  I  I  H  K  I  H  D  K  R  L  E  D
Y  C  K  X  M  X  S  Z  I  E  T  Q  H  X  Z
```

_____ **1.** Chicago   _____ **5.** Denver   _____ **9.** Des Moines

_____ **2.** Gateway Arch   _____ **6.** Grand Canyon _____ **10.** Hood River

_____ **3.** Mount Rushmore _____ **7.** Mount St. Helens _____ **11.** Muir Woods

_____ **4.** Salt Lake City _____ **8.** Santa Fe   _____ **12.** Sitka

26

Unit 3
Multiple Intelligences G4–6, SV 9780547625744

Unit 3: United States Regions—Middle West & West

Build a Diorama

Make a diorama that displays the resources found in the Middle West or the West.

Directions

1. Choose a middle western or western state. Use reference books, the map below, or the Internet to find out what resources and products your state produces.

2. Remove the lid from your shoe box and turn the box on one side. Use construction paper, markers, and glue to decorate the inside of the box so that it represents your state.

3. Draw and cut out the resources and products. Fold and glue them in place to create a scene that shows your state's resources and products.

4. Present your diorama to the class. Explain what natural resources and products your state produces, what they are used for, and why they are important.

Materials:
- construction paper
- reference books
- Internet (optional)
- scissors
- glue
- markers
- shoe box

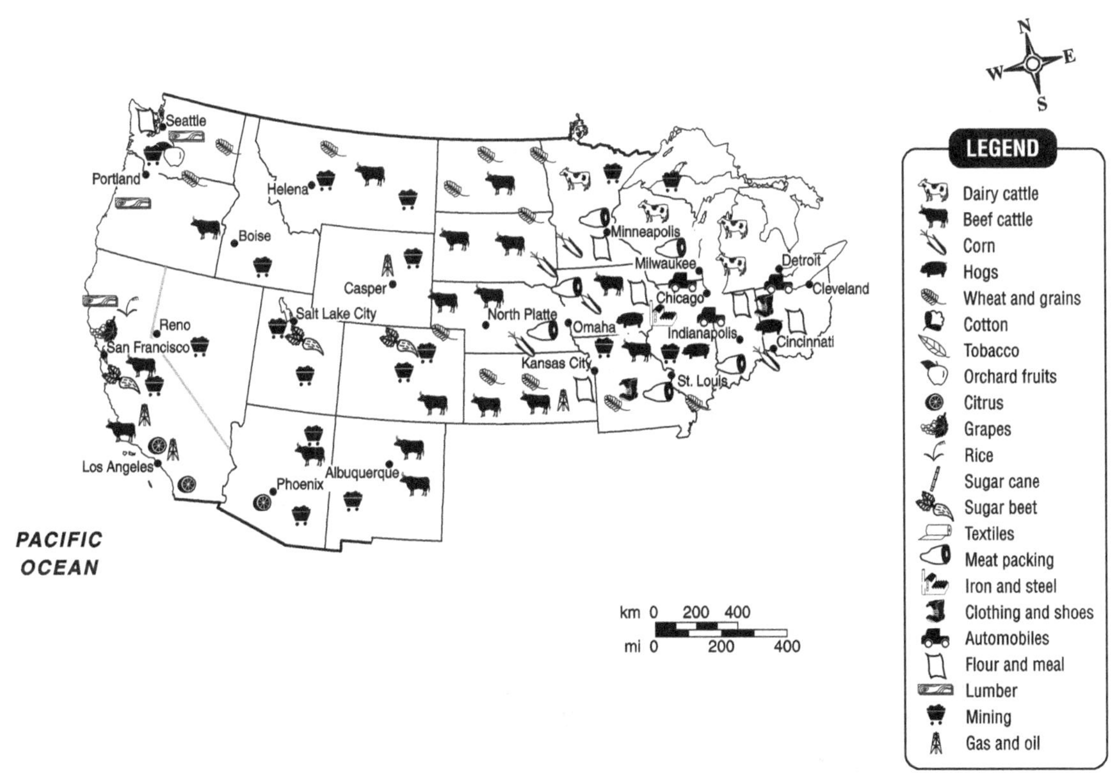

Multiple Intelligences G4–6, SV 9780547625744

Reaching a Consensus

Early Native Americans depended on the land and
other natural resources to survive. If the resources
in an area became scarce, they moved to other
areas where they could survive. What would you
and your classmates do to survive if you lived
back then?

<table>
<tr><td>Materials:</td></tr>
<tr><td>paper</td></tr>
<tr><td>pencil</td></tr>
</table>

Directions

1. Work with a group and study the map below. Discuss the three
   major regions and their food sources as shown on the map.

2. Suppose you and your group members belonged to a Native American
   farming group that lived in the Southwest during the 1600s. A severe
   drought has killed all of the crops in the Southwest region and you have
   nothing to eat. Where should you move?

3. Discuss your two options: 1) Moving into the farming, hunting, and
   gathering region; 2) Moving to the hunting, gathering, and fishing region.

4. Discuss the advantages and disadvantages of each option. Then reach
   a consensus, or an opinion reached by the whole group.

5. Write down reasons to justify your decision. Present your decision and
   reasons to the class.

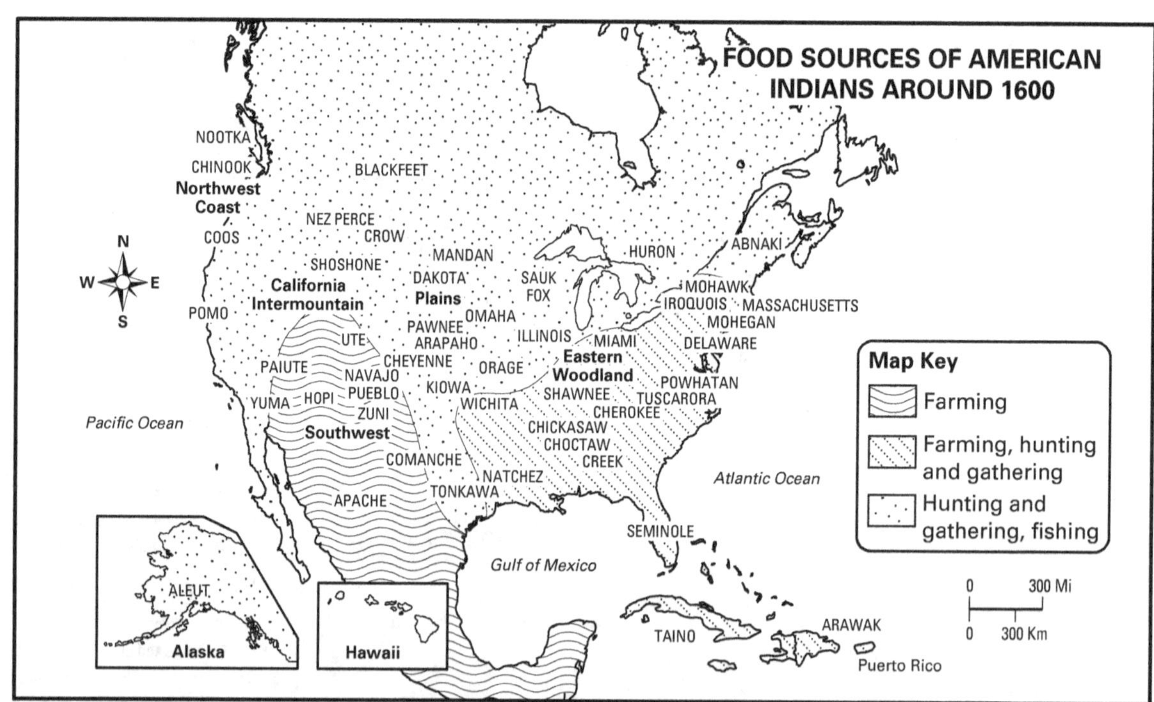

Paint a Picture of a Poem

"Hiawatha" is a famous poem written by Henry Wadsworth Longfellow in 1856. The poem took Longfellow nine months to write and consists of 5,314 lines. The poem tells the story of Hiawatha, a strong leader and subject of Algonquin Indian legend. Listen to the description in the poem and paint a picture of what you visualize.

Materials:

paper (for painting)
paintbrush
paints
jar of water (for rinsing brushes)

Directions

1. Longfellow wrote "Hiawatha" so that each line had eight syllables, with stresses falling on the first, third, fifth, and seventh syllables. Read aloud the excerpt from "Hiawatha" in meter with your class.

2. As your teacher rereads the poem, visualize the scene.

3. Paint a picture of what you see in your mind. Share your artwork when it is dry.

from **Hiawatha**
by Henry Wadsworth Longfellow

On the shore stood Hiawatha,
Turned and waved his hand at parting;
On the clear and luminous water
Launched his birch canoe for sailing,
From the pebbles of the margin
Shoved it forth into the water;
Whispered to it, "Westward! westward!"
And with speed it darted forward.

And the evening sun descending
Set the clouds on fire with redness,
Burned the broad sky, like a prairie,
Left upon the level water
One long track and trail of splendor,
Down whose stream, as down a river,
Westward, westward Hiawatha
Sailed into the fiery sunset,
Sailed into the purple vapors,
Sailed into the dusk of evening:

And the people from the margin
Watched him floating, rising, sinking,
Till the birch canoe seemed lifted
High into that sea of splendor,
Till it sank into the vapors
Like the new moon slowly, slowly
Sinking in the purple distance.

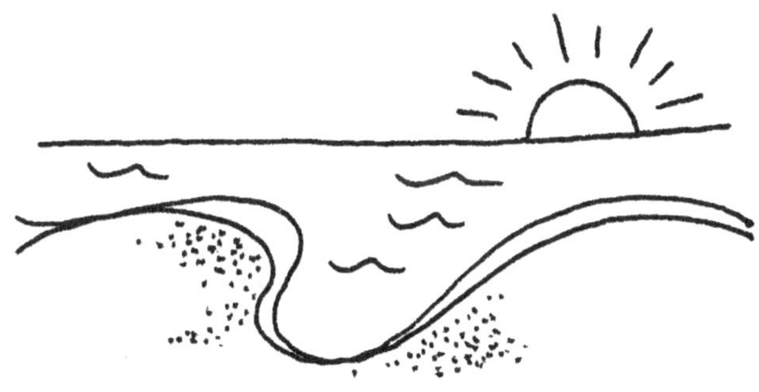

Create Native American Beads

Many early Native Americans made beads from shells and used them to barter, or trade, for other things they needed. They also used shell, wood, or clay beads to decorate clothing, such as belts, vests, and moccasins. Work with a group to make salt clay and beads.

Materials:
1 cup flour
string
1 cup salt
scissors
water
paintbrush
toothpick
paints
paper plate
jar of water
   (for rinsing brushes)
measuring cup

Directions

1. Work in a small group. Mix together 1 cup of flour and 1 cup of salt on a paper plate.

2. Add a small amount of cool water to the flour and salt. Roll together and form a ball.

3. If the ball is sticky, add more flour. If the ball is dry, add more water.

4. Roll small bits of the salt clay into beads and use a toothpick to poke a hole through each bead.

5. Let the beads dry overnight and then paint them. Use your clay beads to barter for other clay beads, if desired.

6. String the beads when you are finished to make a friendship bracelet. Keep your bracelet or give it to a friend.

Play a Native American Game

Native American children played games to help increase their observation skills. Play a pebble game with a partner and test your power of observation.

Directions

1. Work with a partner. Each partner has 30 pebbles and brings them outside. Find a spot free of grass, flowers, or any other obstructions.

2. Sit beside your partner. Cover your eyes while your partner uses about 20 pebbles to make a pattern or a design.

3. Uncover your eyes and study the pattern while your partner counts to 30 silently.

4. After 30 seconds, your partner will cover the pebbles with a towel so that you cannot see the design.

5. Use your pebbles to recreate the design. Uncover the original design to see how closely the two designs match.

6. Switch roles and continue to play. Work up to 30 pebbles and increase the difficulty of the designs.

Materials:
60 pebbles
towel (or anything to cover up a pebble design)
outdoor spot

Unit 4: Land and Early People

Write a Native American Tale

A picture is worth a thousand words. What story might these images tell?

Directions

<table>
<tr><td valign="top">

1. Study each of the pictures below. Write a few sentences that describe what might have happened before, during, and after the moment each picture captures.

2. Write a Native American tale that incorporates the actions of one, two, or all three of the pictures.

3. Read your story to a partner. Listen as your partner reads to you.

</td></tr>
</table>

<table>
<tr><td>

Materials: ______________

paper

pencil

</td></tr>
</table>

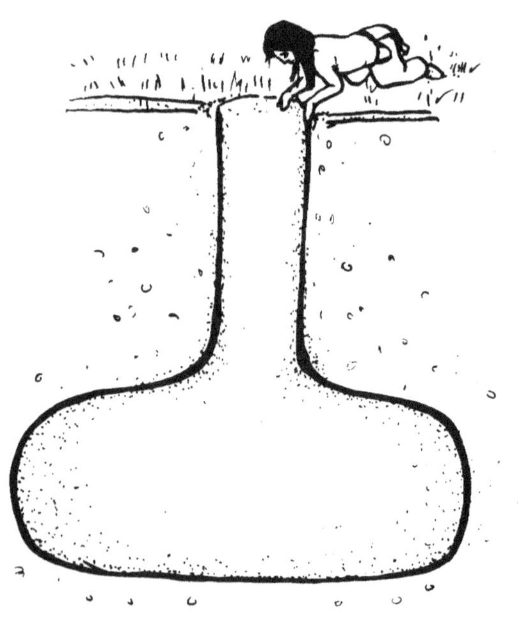

Multiple Intelligences G4–6, SV 9780547625744

Make a Birchbark Canoe

Native Americans who lived in the northern New England region made canoes from the bark of birch trees. Make your own birchbark canoe.

Directions

1. Fold a piece of construction in paper in half lengthwise. The fold should be facing up and the edges of the construction paper should be facing down.

2. Make another fold about half an inch from the original fold line. The fold should be facing down. Do the same on the other side. Both edges of the construction paper should be facing up. Now you have made an accordion fold on the bottom of the canoe.

3. Draw a canoe shape on one side of the construction paper. Make sure the folds are on the bottom of the canoe.

4. Cut out the canoe. Make sure not to cut along the bottom of the canoe. Use a hole punch to make holes on each end of the canoe.

5. Weave yarn through the holes on each side of the canoe and tie knots.

6. Push the folded floor down to make the canoe sit flat on the table.

Materials:

brown construction paper
scissors
hole punch
yarn

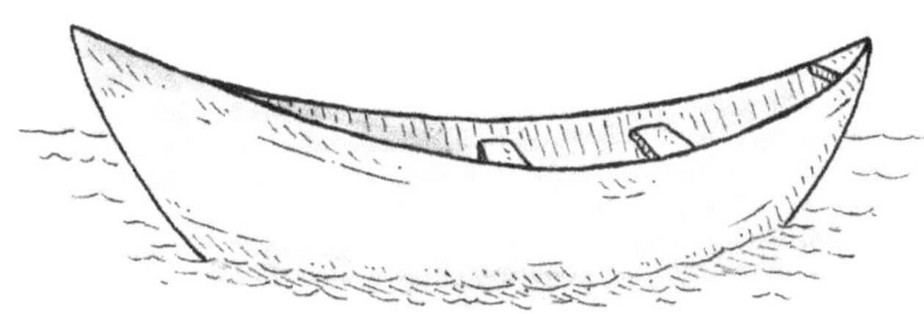

Imitate Inuit Throat-Singing

The Inuits live in icy regions, such as Alaska and Canada. Throat singing is an Inuit style of singing in which two singers try to show their vocal talents. Try throat singing with a partner!

Directions

1. Throat singing is a singing contest between two people. First, face your partner. Decide who will be the leader and who will be the follower.

2. The leader sings in a pattern of high and low throat noises. The leader leaves silent gaps in between some of the throat noises.

3. The follower listens to the leader and quickly fills in the gaps with his or her own throat noises.

4. A singer wins when the other one runs out of breath, laughs, or cannot keep up with the pace of the game.

5. Switch roles and throat-sing again!

Design a Lakota Winter Count

The Lakota Sioux kept a pictorial calendar to keep track of events. This calendar was called a winter count. A "winter," or year, was measured from first snowfall to first snowfall. Winter counts were traditionally drawn on buffalo hides and often run in spirals. The pictures helped the Lakota people remember past events.

Materials:
brown paper bag
markers or colored
    pencils
scissors

Directions

1. Cut out a paper bag into a buffalo hide shape. Tear off the cut edges so that the buffalo hide looks ragged.

2. Wrinkle and unwrinkle the paper several times until it looks worn.

3. Imagine that you are the winter count recorder for a Lakota tribe who is recording ten years of the tribe's history. Choose one symbol to represent a significant event for each year. You can use the symbols below or make up ones of your own. Write a few sentences describing the significance of each of the events and how it affected your tribe.

4. Place your first symbol in the center of your paper. Then draw the other symbols around the first symbol to make a large spiral pattern.

5. Join others to form a small group. Take turns explaining what each of the symbols in your winter count stands for and sharing the histories.

Tell a Nature Story

Early Native Americans used storytelling to explain how things in nature came to be, such as how a mighty warrior made fire from the sun. Tell a story to your classmates about why something in nature exists.

Materials:

pencil

paper

quiet outdoor spot

Directions

1. Sit is a small circle outside. Look at the nature around you to get ideas for your story and choose a natural element or object to write a story about. Once you have selected a topic, spend a few minutes writing down a short story that explains how the natural element or object was created or why it exists.

2. When everyone is finished, decide who will go first.

3. Take turns telling stories.

Give a Speech

During the 1700s, American colonists wanted to be free from King George III's rule. The colonists wanted the freedom to make their own laws. They did not want to pay taxes to the British government. Many colonists spoke out against the injustices, but others were fearful. Suppose you were a colonist. What would you say to convince others to stand up to King George III?

> **Materials:**
> paper
> pencil

Directions

1. Think about the following questions:

   - How do you feel about the British government making laws for you to follow?

   - How do you feel about these laws being made without your consent?

   - Why do you think it is important for the colonists to govern themselves?

   - Do you think it is necessary to follow King George III's decisions? Explain.

   - How do you feel about the presence of British soldiers in the colonies?

   - How do you think the money you pay to the British government is being used?

2. Jot down your answers on a sheet of paper. Use your ideas to write a persuasive speech. Tell why it is important to speak up for your rights as a colonist.

3. Use persuasive words such as *should*, *must*, and *ought* to sound more convincing.

4. Write down what you would like to say. Practice reading your speech aloud.

5. Sit in a group with others. Stand when it is your turn to speak. Use good eye contact. Speak persuasively. Use gestures.

6. Listen when others give their speeches.

Analyze a Political Cartoon

A political cartoon is a cartoon that expresses a political or social message. A political cartoon often uses symbols to give an opinion and explain complicated political issues. What message do you think this political cartoon conveys about the struggle between the American colonists and the British government after the French and Indian War?

Directions

1. Discuss the following situation with your group: In 1763 Great Britain and France signed a treaty that ended the French and Indian War. The cost of the war greatly increased Great Britain's debt. In order to recover economically, the British Parliament decided to raise taxes.

2. Study the cartoon and discuss the following questions:

   a. Look at the Atlantic Ocean. What land is shown on either side?

   b. Who does the man on the right represent? What is he holding in each hand? Why does he have a bad leg and a crutch? What symbol do you see underneath his crutch?

   c. Who are the people on the left? Why are they attached to strings? Who is controlling them? How do they feel?

   d. What is the cartoon's message? Do you think the cartoonist was a colonist? Explain.

Name ______________________________   Date ______________

Write a Descriptive Paragraph

On December 16, 1773, the American colonists developed a plan to fight against Great Britain's heavy taxation. The latest tax, a tea tax, caused outrage among the colonists. When three tea ships arrived in Boston, the colonists planned to dispose of the cargo.

Materials:
paper
pencil

The colonists dressed like Indians and boarded the ships. They whooped like Indians and threw the crates of tea overboard into the Boston harbor. This event became known as the Boston Tea Party. Suppose you were a colonist who witnessed the scene below. How would you describe it to others who were not there to witness it?

Directions

1. Look at the picture below. Study what each man is doing. What do you see?

2. Imagine the sounds you would hear. Think about the smell of tea filling the air.

3. Use your senses and what you see in the picture to write a description of the Boston Tea Party for other colonists who were not able to witness the event.

4. Find a partner and take turns reading your descriptions. Discuss how the descriptions are alike and how they are different.

39

Create a Silhouette Portrait

Silhouette portraits were common during colonial times. Create a silhouette portrait of yourself and then write about your life as if you were living in colonial America.

Directions

1. Tape a large piece of black construction paper to the wall. Make sure to position the paper so that there is enough room to outline both your profile and a colonial hairstyle like the ones shown below.

2. Stand close to the wall and turn sideways. Close your eyes as you have a partner face you and turn on a flashlight.

3. Hold still as your partner draws an outline of your profile. Switch roles.

4. Draw a colonial hairstyle on your silhouette. Cut out the silhouette and glue it pencil side down to the white piece of construction paper.

5. On the back, write your name and a brief description about your life in colonial times. Are you a blacksmith, printer, or plantation owner? Do you cook for your family or churn butter? Which colony do you live in? How do you feel about King George III?

6. Display your silhouette on the wall with those of other classmates. Take turns guessing which classmate is depicted in each portrait. Once your portrait is correctly identified, read the back of the portrait to your classmates.

> **Materials:**
> - flashlight (or another light source)
> - black construction paper (large)
> - white construction paper (large)
> - pencil

Multiple Intelligences G4–6, SV 9780547625744

Make Butter as You Sing

Colonial women had to make many things their family needed. They made and mended clothing, cooked food, made candles, and churned butter. Make your own butter with a group as you sing a colonial song.

Directions

1. Pour enough whipping cream into a baby food jar to fill it about 2/3 full.

2. Take turns shaking the jar for 5 minutes as you sing "Yankee Doodle."

3. Keep shaking until the whipping cream forms one solid chunk. Spread the butter on crackers or bread and enjoy!

Materials:

- 1 clean baby food jar per group (chilled, if possible)
- crackers or small pieces of bread
- plastic knife
- napkins
- whipping cream (chilled, if possible)

YANKEE DOODLE

Father and I went down to camp
Along with Captain Gooding
And there we saw the men and boys
As thick as hasty pudding.

Chorus: Yankee Doodle, keep it up
Yankee Doodle dandy
Mind the music and the step
And with the girls be handy

And there we saw a thousand men,
As rich as Squire David;
And what they wasted every day,
I wish it could be saved.

Chorus: Yankee Doodle, keep it up
Yankee Doodle dandy
Mind the music and the step
And with the girls be handy

There was Captain Washington
Upon a slapping stallion
A-giving orders to his men
I guess there was a million.

Chorus: Yankee Doodle, keep it up
Yankee Doodle dandy
Mind the music and the step
And with the girls be handy

Unit 5: The American Revolution

Interpreting Graphs

Graphs are useful tools for helping you understand information. When you interpret a graph, you are better able to evaluate information and draw conclusions. Look at Graph A and Graph B below. They give you different sets information about the Revolutionary War. Read the directions below and then create a chart.

> **Materials:**
> paper
> pencil
> reference books
> Internet (optional)

Directions

1. Make a four-column chart on a separate sheet of paper. Label the columns as follows: Colony, Number of Battles, Year, and Name of Battle

2. In Column 1, list the colonies shown in Graph A.

3. In Column 2, list the number of battles shown in Graph A.

4. Look at the number of battles that occurred in each year shown on Graph B.

5. Use reference books or the Internet to research the names of the battles that happened in each year shown on Graph B. Make sure to also find out in which colony the battle took place.

6. Write the year and the name of each battle in the correct place in Columns 3 and 4.

7. Find a partner and compare charts. Correct any discrepancies.

Graph A

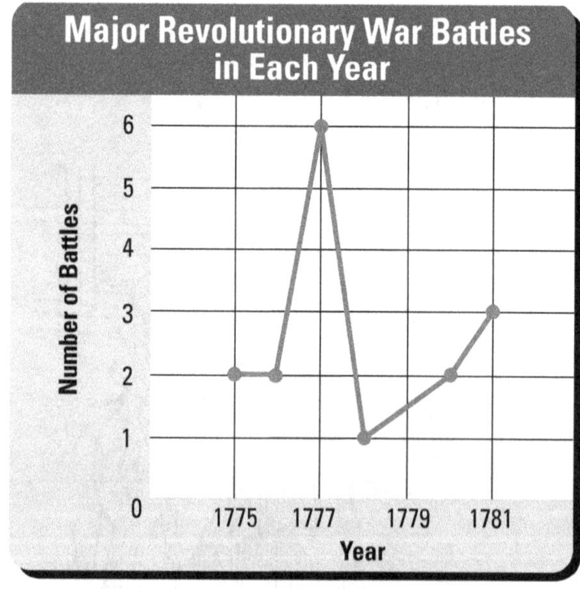

Graph B

42
Unit 5
Multiple Intelligences G4–6, SV 9780547625744

Map Paul Revere's Ride

Draw a map of Paul Revere's ride based on the information in the poem "The Midnight Ride of Paul Revere."

Materials:
map of the colonies
pencil
drawing paper
colored pencils

Directions

1. Read an excerpt from "Paul Revere's Ride" with your group. Clap to the beat as though it is the sound of a horse's hooves.

2. Use a map of the colonies to reproduce the basic shape and borders on a sheet of drawing paper.

3. Then use the information in the poem to draw Paul Revere's route. Revere's journey began in Charlestown. Label the places mentioned in the poem and color your map. Display your map.

from **Paul Revere's Ride**
by Henry Wadsworth Longfellow

It was twelve by the village clock,
When he crossed the bridge into Medford
   town.
He heard the crowing of the cock,
And the barking of the farmer's dog,
And felt the damp of the river fog
That rises after the sun goes down.

It was one by the village clock,
When he galloped into Lexington.
He saw the gilded weathercock
Swim in the moonlight as he passed,
And the meeting-house windows blank
   and bare,
Gaze at him with a spectral glare,
As if they already stood aghast
At the bloody work they would look upon.

It was two by the village clock,
When he came to the bridge in Concord
   town.

He heard the bleating of the flock,
And the twitter of birds among the trees,
And felt the breath of the morning breeze
Blowing over the meadows brown.
And one was safe and asleep in his bed
Who at the bridge would be first to fall,
Who that day would be lying dead,
Pierced by a British musket-ball.

You know the rest. In the books you have
   read,
How the British Regulars fired and fled, —
How the farmers gave them ball for ball,
From behind each fence and farmyard
   wall,
Chasing the red-coats down the lane,
Then crossing the fields to emerge again
Under the trees at the turn of the road,
And only pausing to fire and load.

Bake Colonial Brown Sugar Cookies

Do you wonder what colonial food tastes like? Try your hand at baking colonial cookies with your group to find out.

Directions

1. In a large bowl mix together the brown sugar, shortening, egg, nutmeg and salt. Add the flour, baking soda, baking powder, and sour cream. Mix well.

2. Take turns dropping spoonfuls of the cookie dough onto a greased baking sheet. Bake 12-15 minutes at 325° degrees. Eat colonial style!

Materials:

use of an oven

large mixing bowl

1 teaspoon

1 tablespoon

measuring cup

napkins

1 c. brown sugar

1 c. shortening

1 egg

1/2 tsp. nutmeg

1/2 tsp. salt

2 c. flour

1/2 tsp. baking soda

2 tsp. baking powder

1/2 c. sour cream

Multiple Intelligences G4–6, SV 9780547625744

Supporting Our Troops

In the winter of 1777, George Washington's Continental Army set up camp in Valley Forge. During the winter, soldiers suffered from bitter cold, hunger, and extreme discomfort. Many soldiers became sick or discouraged. Write a letter of support, encouragement, and thanks to a soldier in the Continental Army.

Materials:
paper
pencil
envelope
reference books
Internet (optional)

Directions

1. Research what conditions were like for soldiers at Valley Forge in the winter of 1777. Imagine what soldiers were feeling and experiencing.

2. Write a letter to a soldier encouraging him to get through the winter and keep fighting. Be sure to thank the soldier for his sacrifices and give him hope for a final victory.

3. Place your letter in an envelope and exchange letters with a partner.

Create an Ancient Civilizations Mobile

Ancient civilizations are the building blocks of
the modern world. Work with a group to make
a mobile that tells about the eight ancient
civilizations listed below.

Phoenician	Egyptian	Babylonian
Greek	Roman	Mayan
Aztec	Sumerian	

Materials:

8 index cards

pencil

colored pencils

yarn

hole punch

hanger

reference books

Internet (optional)

Directions

1. Work in a group of four to make a mobile. Each member chooses two ancient
   civilizations from the list above and creates two index cards to hang from the mobile.

2. Use the Internet or reference books to find out about your two ancient civilizations.

3. On the front of each of your index cards, write a paragraph about your ancient
   civilization. Include the location, dates of existence, and 3-5 interesting facts.

4. On the back of each of your index cards, illustrate
   a scene from your ancient civilization.

5. Punch a hole in the tops of your index cards.
   Thread yarn through each hole and fasten
   your index cards to the hanger.

6. When your group is finished, read through
   the facts so that everyone learns about
   the eight ancient civilizations. Then
   present your mobile to another group.
   Listen as they present theirs.

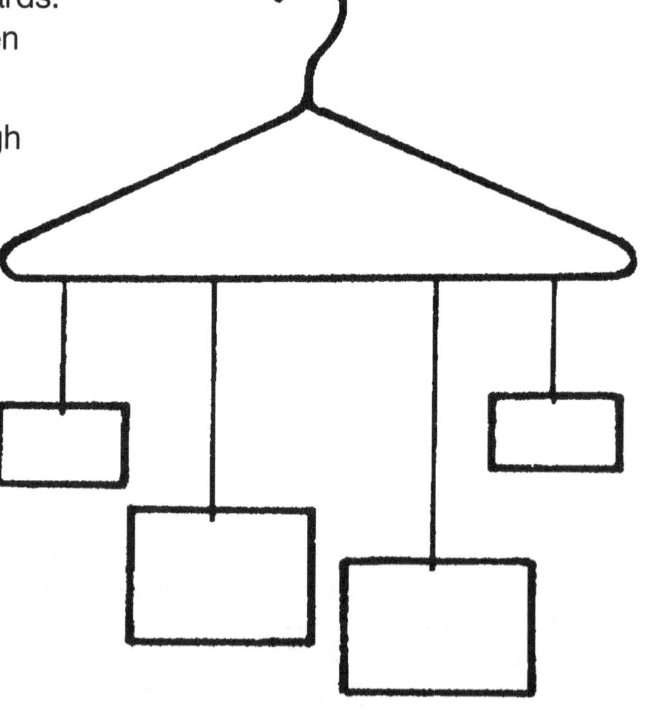

Build a Sumerian Ziggurat

Sumeria was an ancient empire of Mesopotamia. Sumeria was located in what is now modern Iraq. Sumerians built ziggurats, which were different from Egyptian pyramids. While the Egyptians had access to stone, the Sumerians were limited to clay. They could not build a hollow pyramid from clay or it would collapse. Instead, they used fired brick. Ziggurats did not have straight walls. Sumerian architects created interesting shapes that allowed light and dark patterns to form on the sides of the ziggurat.

Materials:
- cardboard
- pen
- tape
- scissors
- ruler

Directions

1. Work in a small group to design a ziggurat similar in size and shape to the one below.

2. Measure the dimensions of the ziggurat below as a guide for building your model.

3. Use your measurements to cut and tape the cardboard sides into place.

4. Use a pen to add detail to your ziggurat.

5. Display your ziggurat.

  Multiple Intelligences G4–6, SV 9780547625744

Compute Using Mayan Math

The Mayan civilization was located in what is now modern day Southeastern Mexico, Guatemala, Belize, Honduras, and El Salvador. The Mayan number system can be traced back the fourth century. The Mayans used a combination of dots and dashes to represent numbers. For example, a series of dots was used to represent the numbers 1–4 and a dash represented the number 5. The Mayans were the first to use the concept of nothing (0), which they represented with a clam shape.

> **Materials:**
> outdoor spot
> 5 sticks
> 4 pebbles
> 1 large rock

Directions

1. Take your pebbles, sticks, and large rock outside, if you already have them. Otherwise, collect them when you are outside. (Pebbles represent dots, sticks represent dashes, and the large rock represents zero.)

2. Sit in a circle with two or three classmates. Use your sticks, rocks, and pebbles to build the following numbers: 3, 4, 6, 8, and 9.

3. Use the numbers below to help you. When everyone is finished, compare answers.

4. Take turns calling out an addition, subtraction, multiplication, or division problem. Use only the numbers 0–20. For example, you could use the following problem: $20 \div 4$.

5. After the caller has stated the problem, members solve the problem and cover their solutions with their hands.

6. Once everyone has solved the problem, uncover the answers and compare solutions.

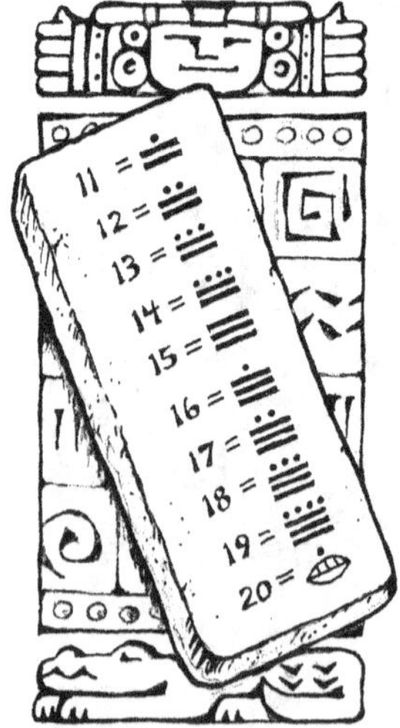

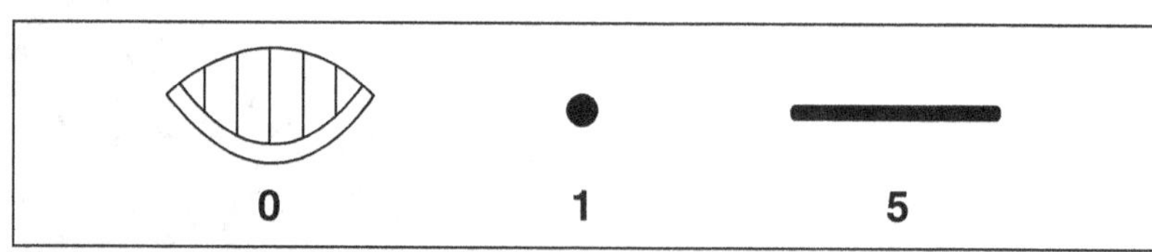

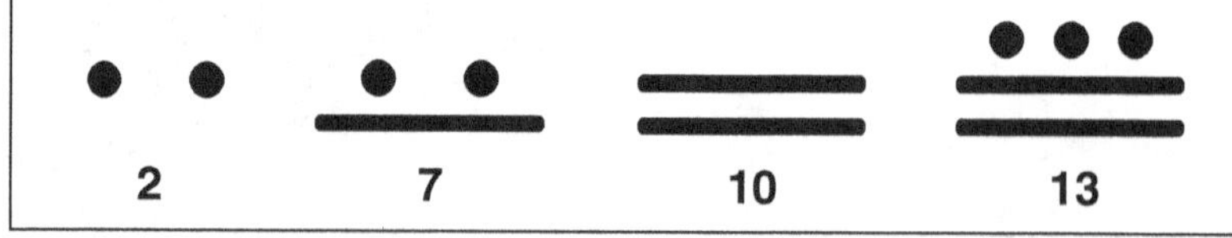

Write Your Own Greek Myth

The ancient Greeks told myths about gods, goddesses, and mortals. These characters had superhuman strengths and talents. Below are a few characters from Greek myths. Read a Greek myth of your choice. Then write a myth of your own.

> **Materials:**
> paper
> pencil
> Greek myths

Directions

1. Below are the elements of a Greek myth:

   - Explains something in nature or the creation of something

   - Shows a struggle between good and evil characters

   - Often shows a hero as he or she attempts to accomplish a goal

2. Read two or three short Greek myths, such as *Pandora's Box*, *Jason and the Golden Fleece*, and *Echo and Narcissus*.

3. Choose a character from Greek mythology as the main character for your story. Ask yourself:

   - What does he or she look like?

   - What is he or she trying to do?

   - What character traits does he or she have?

   - Who stands in his or her way?

4. Use the elements of a Greek myth as a model to write your own myth.

5. Read your myth aloud to the class.

Make Natural Dye

The ancient Phoenicians lived in what is now modern Lebanon. The Phoenicians were famous for their purple dye, which was made from the secretion of sea snails, and beautiful cloth. Work with your classmates to make your own dye.

Directions

1. Put on a pair of disposable plastic gloves. Then place a large mixing bowl on top of several paper towels.

2. Place the blueberries in the bowl and mash them with a potato masher. Add 1 tbsp. of water to thin the blueberry mixture and stir.

3. Strain the blueberry juice from the mixture into a small bowl.

4. Add 1 tbsp. of white vinegar to the blueberry liquid and stir well.

5. Soak the white cloth in the blueberry liquid for 30 minutes.

6. Pick out the cloth and squeeze it over the bowl.

7. Lay your purple cloth on a stack of paper towels or hang it outside to dry.

Materials:

- 2 c. blueberries
- 1 tbsp. water
- 1 tbsp. white vinegar
- small bowl
- disposable plastic gloves
- large mixing bowl
- tablespoon
- strainer
- piece of white cloth (muslin, linen, or cotton)
- paper towels
- potato masher

Multiple Intelligences G4–6, SV 9780547625744

Research the Hanging Gardens of Babylon

The Hanging Gardens of Babylon were one of the Seven Wonders of the Ancient World. According to legend, a Babylonian king had the terraced gardens built for his wife. The Hanging Gardens were supposedly located in the royal palace at Babylon, in what is now southern Iraq.

Materials:
reference books
Internet (optional)
crayons or colored
  pencils
drawing paper

Directions

1. Use reference books or the Internet to research the Hanging Gardens of Babylon. Take notes on a sheet of paper. Describe the gardens in as much detail as possible.

2. On your drawing paper, sketch and color a picture of the Hanging Gardens based on your research.

3. Use your notes to write a descriptive paragraph about the Hanging Gardens of Babylon on the back of the paper.

4. Share your work in a small group.

Make an Egyptian Harp

Music was an important part of ancient Egyptian culture. Egyptian hieroglyphics often show people playing musical instruments, such as rattles, drums, flutes, and harps. Now you can make your own Egyptian harp.

Directions

1. Cut a 4 or 5 square-inch hole in the lid of a shoe box.

2. Cut two jagged pieces from the corrugated cardboard as shown below.

3. Have your teacher use a glue gun to glue the two jagged pieces in place. One of the jagged pieces should be angled while the other one should be straight.

4. Use markers to draw pictures or hieroglyphics on the shoe box.

5. Stretch rubber bands from one side to the other as shown in the picture.

6. Practice playing and singing songs on your harp.

Materials:

shoe box and lid

scissors

corrugated cardboard

glue gun

rubber bands

markers

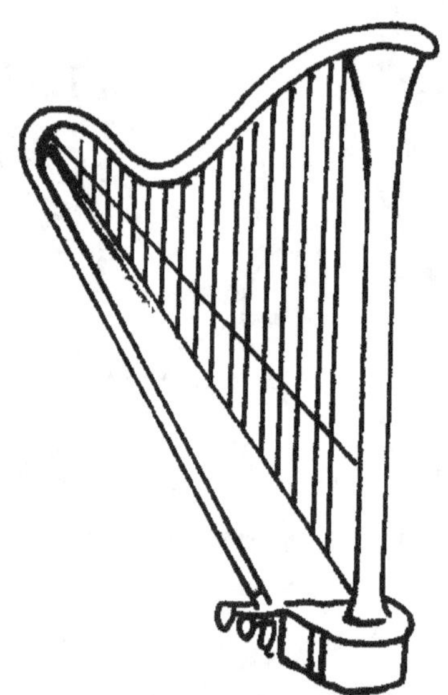

Unit 6
Multiple Intelligences G4–6, SV 9780547625744

Athenian Acropolis

In ancient Greek cities, important religious and government buildings were often built on the highest ground in the city—the acropolis. The Acropolis in Athens, Greece, is the most famous acropolis in Greece. Research the ancient buildings located on the Athenian acropolis to find out more about Athen's fascinating history.

Materials:
paper
pencil
reference books
Internet (optional)

Directions

1. Study the drawing of the Acropolis in Athens. This image depicts what the buildings would have looked like in ancient times.

2. Use reference books or the Internet to research the Acropolis and label the important structures on the drawing below.

3. Circle the structures that are still visible on the modern-day Acropolis site. On a separate sheet of paper, write brief descriptions of each of these structures.

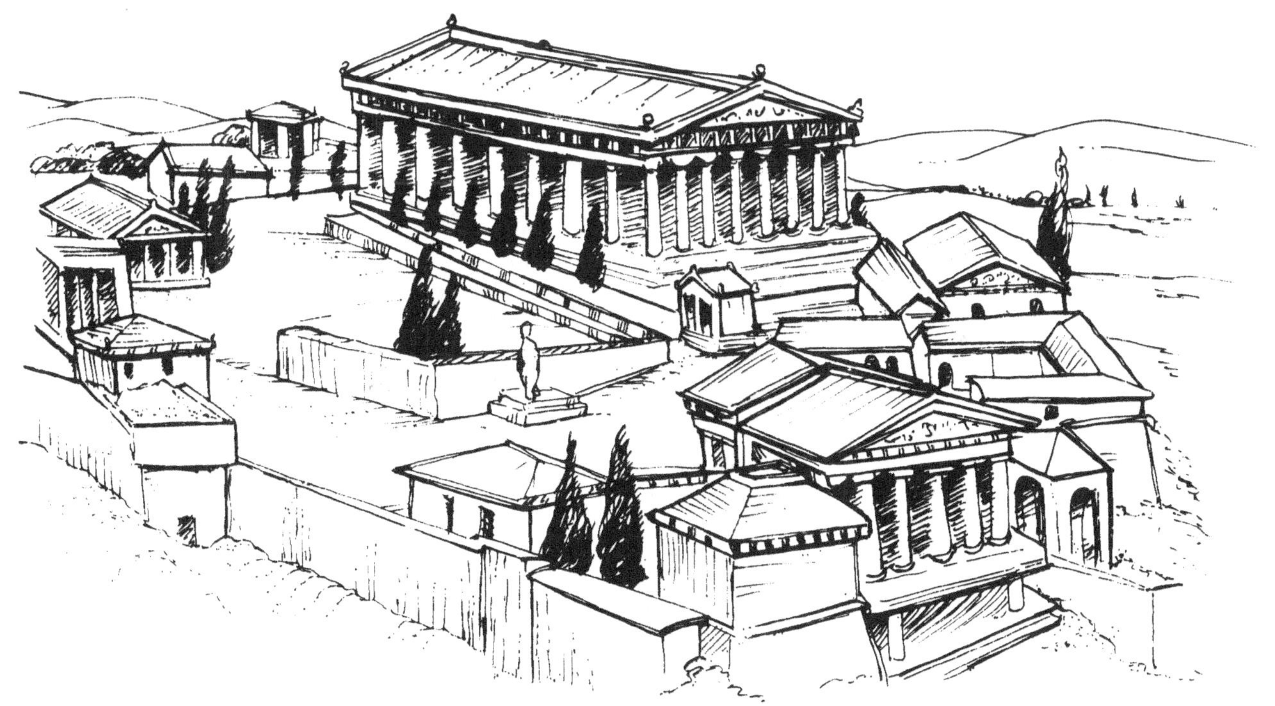

53

Analyze Maps of Ancient Rome

Study the two maps of ancient Rome. Look at the time period, key, and the symbols. What changes occurred over time?

Directions

1. Study the maps below and make notes about the following features:

   - the length of aqueducts (manmade structures for carrying water)

   - the number and location of buildings

   - the road system

2. On a separate sheet of paper, write a paragraph about the changes over time, based on the maps. Use the information to draw conclusions about the changes in ancient Rome over 400 years.

Materials:

paper

pencil

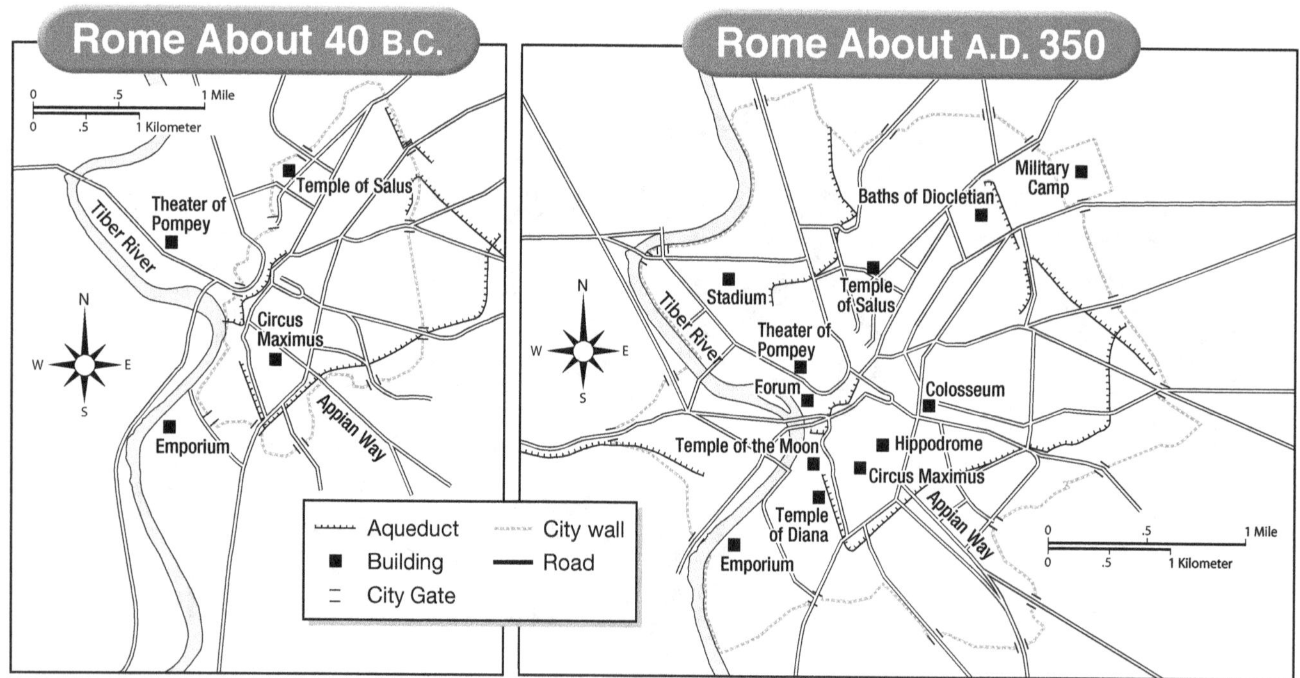

54

Be an Expert

**Australia is divided into seven different regions.
How much do you know about them?**

Directions

1. Work in a group of five to cut apart the five pieces.
   (The rectangular piece contains three regions that
   should not be cut apart.) Each member takes a
   piece of Australia and a colored pencil.

2. Use reference books or the Internet to find out
   more about your region, including the major cities,
   landforms, types of animals, and interesting places.

3. Use the information to draw symbols and label your piece. Then
   use your colored pencil to lightly shade the entire region.

4. Take turns presenting pieces and sharing facts to the other group
   members. Then glue the pieces together on a sheet of drawing paper.

Materials:

pencil
reference books
Internet (optional)
colored pencils
drawing paper
glue

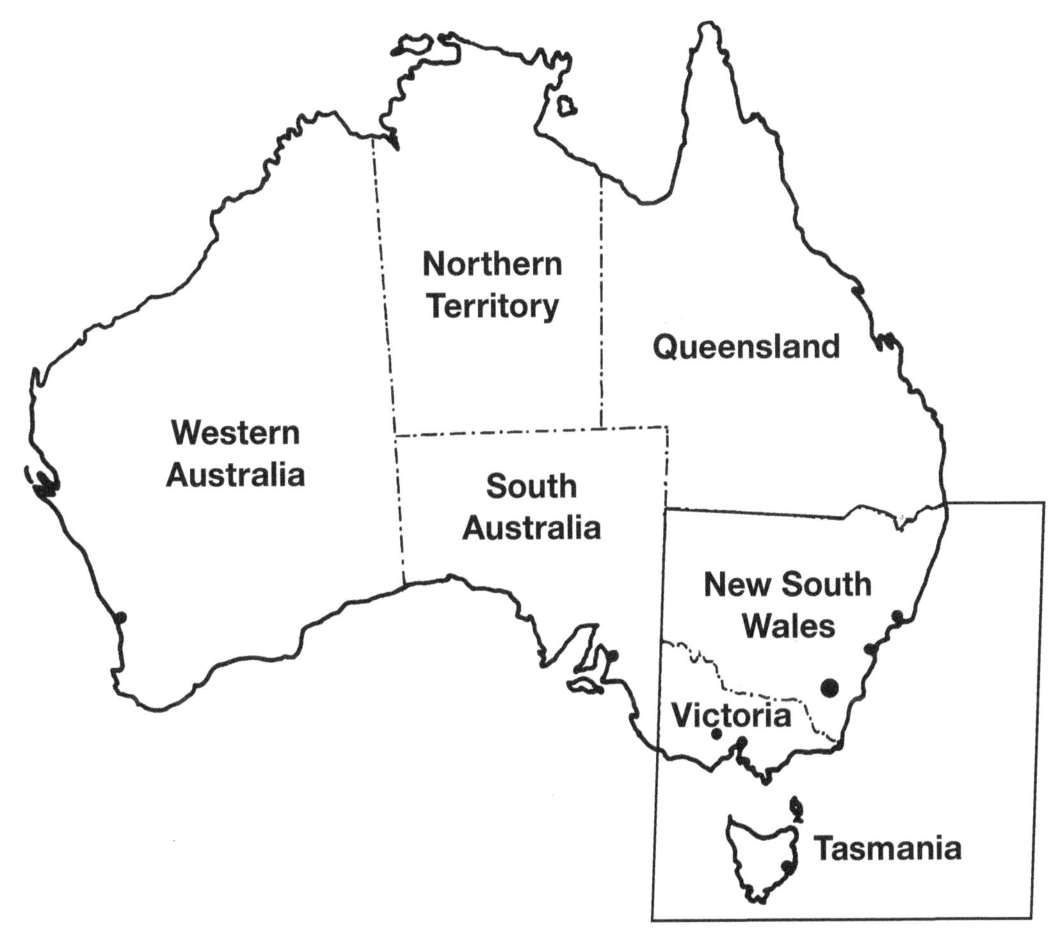

Acrostic Animals

Acrostic poems are fun to write. Choose an Australian animal and write an acrostic poem that describes your animal. Examples of animals include the following: kangaroo, koala, dingo, duck-billed platypus, kookaburra, wombat, emu, sugar glider, echidna.

Materials:

pencil
drawing paper
markers or colored pencils
reference books
Internet (optional)

Directions

1. Choose an Australian animal. Use reference books or the Internet to conduct research to find out more about it.

2. Write the letters of the animal's name on a sheet of drawing paper and use each letter to begin a phrase that describes the animal. An example has been provided.

3. Illustrate and color your acrostic poem and share it with others.

Make a Didgeridoo

The didgeridoo is a traditional Australian instrument first played by Australian aborigines. It is a long tube with a narrow mouthpiece and makes a low humming or buzzing sound when played.

Directions

1. Tape two paper towel tubes together with masking tape to make one long tube.

2. Cut enough drawing paper to cover the tube without overlapping the edges.

3. Use markers to make designs on the drawing paper. Then wrap the paper around the tube and tape it in place with clear tape.

4. Pretend to play your didgeridoo. Your teacher may have a recording of didgeridoo music. If so, listen to the different sounds.

Materials:

markers
clear tape
masking tape
drawing paper
2 paper towel tubes
didgeridoo music
   (if possible)

The didgeridoo is an Australian aboriginal instrument.

Sing "Waltzing Matilda"

The Song "Waltzing Matilda" is a famous Australia song about a man who wanders (waltzing) in the wilderness with his bag of belongings (matilda).

Directions

1. Sit outside in a circle with your classmates. Sing "Waltzing Matilda." Then read the definitions of the Australian words used in the song.

2. Sing the song again, this time using gestures to act out the song.

Waltzing Matilda

Oh! there once was a swagman camped in
   a Billabong,
Under the shade of a Coolibah tree;
And he sang as he lookd up at his billy
   boiling,
"Who'll come a-waltzing Matilda with me?"

Chorus: Who'll come a-waltzingMatilda,
   my darling,
Who'll come a-waltzing Matilda with me?
Waltzing Matilda and leading a water-bag—
Who'll come a-waltzing Matilda with me?

Down came a jumbuck to drink at the
   water-hole;
Up jumped the swagman a grabbed him
   in glee;
And he sang as he stowed him away in his
   tucker-bag,
"You'll come a-waltzing Matilda with me!"

Repeat Chorus

Down came the Squatter a-riding his
   thoroughbred;
Down came Policemen—one, two and
   three.
"Whose is the jumbuck you've got in the
   tucker-bag?
You'll come a-waltzing Matilda with me."

Repeat Chorus

But the swagman, he up and he jumped in
   the water-hole,
Drowning himself by the Coolibah tree;
And his ghost may be heard as it sings in
   the Billabong;
"Who'll come a-waltzing Matilda with me?"

- Billabong: a waterhole
- Billy: a small kettle used to boil water.
- Coolibah tree: a type of native tree in Australia
- Jumbuck: a sheep
- Matilda: belongings rolled into a swag and tossed over the shoulders
- Squatter: someone who lives on another person's land without permission
- Swagman: Someone who lives on the open road
- Tucker-bag: a bag for storing food in the wilderness.

A Talking Statue

Easter Island is an island in the South Pacific. Easter Island is world famous for its 887 mysterious large stone statues. These statues were built by the Rapa Nui people during the Stone Age. People often wonder why these statues were built and how they were able to be moved.

Directions

1. Suppose you are one of the huge statues that guards Easter Island. Write about why the Rapa Nui people built you and how they were able to move you to the edge of the island.

2. Read your paper aloud to a partner. Use expression when you speak.

____

____

____

____

____

____

____

____

Multiple Intelligences G4–6, SV 9780547625744

South Pacific Dream Island Vacation

The South Pacific is dotted with beautiful islands. Imagine that your family has just won a dream vacation to the South Pacific. All you to have to do is choose your destination and pack your bags. Which destination will you choose?

Materials:

paper

pencil

reference books

Internet (optional)

Directions

1. Review the list of South Pacific island destinations. Choose the one you would like to visit for your Dream Island Vacation. (If you are not sure which island you would like to visit, do a little preliminary research first and choose the one that looks most interesting.)

2. Use reference books or the Internet to research your destination.

   - How many islands make up the destination country?

   - What are some popular tourist activities at your destination?

   - What language is spoken there?

   - How many people live there?

3. Write a letter to the contest sponsor in which you identify where you will go on your vacation, what you've learned about your destination, and what you plan to do on your dream vacation.

4. Exchange letters with someone who chose a different destination and read about another South Pacific island destination.

Dream Island Vacation

Pack your bags!

Your family has just won an all-expense-paid trip to the South Pacific. Choose your destination from the list below.

Fiji	**Cook Islands**
Papua New Guinea	**Tahiti**
Marshall Islands	**Solomon Islands**
Samoa	

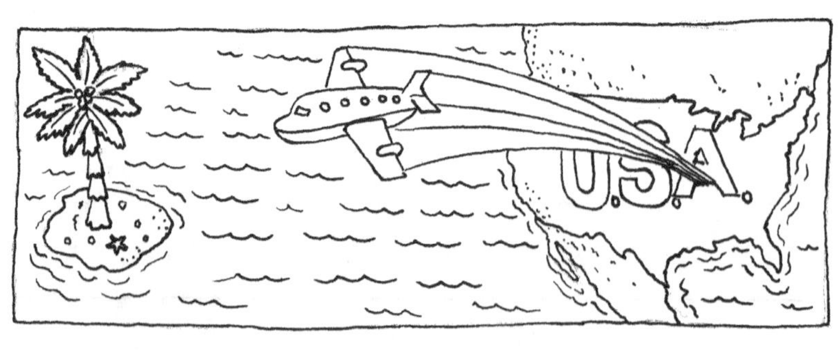

Multiple Intelligences G4–6, SV 9780547625744

Create a Sidewalk Mural of Australia

Australia is home to many interesting natural and manmade landmarks. Research the landmarks below and then create a sidewalk mural picturing Australia's unique landmarks and locations.

Sydney Opera House	Uluru/Ayers Rock
Shark Bay	Great Barrier Reef
The Twelve Apostles	Lake Eyre
Port Arthur	Wave Rock

Materials:

sidewalk
sidewalk chalk
reference books
Internet (optional)
map of Australia

Directions

1. As a class, locate a large section of sidewalk or concrete that you can easily and safely draw on. Appoint one member of the class to draw a large outline of Australia.

2. Divide the class into 8 groups. Each group will choose one of the landmarks listed above to research and label on the mural. Use reference books or the Internet to find out the answers to the following questions:

   - Where is the landmark located?

   - What are its distinguishing features?

3. Once your group completes its research, choose an image to represent your landmark on the sidewalk mural. Appoint one person to mark the location and draw the image on the mural.

4. When all groups have added their landmarks to the mural, take turns presenting the information you learned to the other groups.

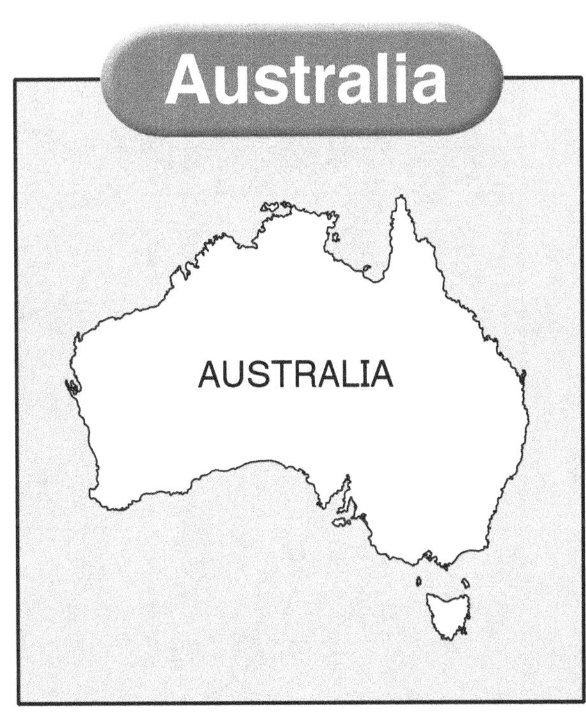

Hooping the Islands

The islands of Oceania are divided into three main groups: Polynesia, Micronesia, and Melanesia. Find out how these regions compare to one another.

Directions

1. As a class, find an empty outdoor spot. Arrange the three hoop rings in a Venn diagram pattern as shown below.

2. Choose one classmate to write in marker the following regions on three index cards: Polynesia, Micronesia, Melanesia.

3. Place each index card in a separate hoop where there is no overlap. Use rocks or blocks as paperweights to keep the index cards from blowing away.

4. As a class, use reference books and maps to find similarities and differences among the three regions.

5. As you find one, write it down on a index card and read it aloud to the class. Place it in the correct spot in the Venn diagram.

6. See how many index cards your class can place in each section of the Venn diagram. When your class has finished, choose members to read aloud the index cards that are grouped together.

> **Materials:**
> 3 large toy hoop rings
> index cards
> markers
> rocks (or blocks) as paperweights
> empty outdoor spot
> reference books
> maps

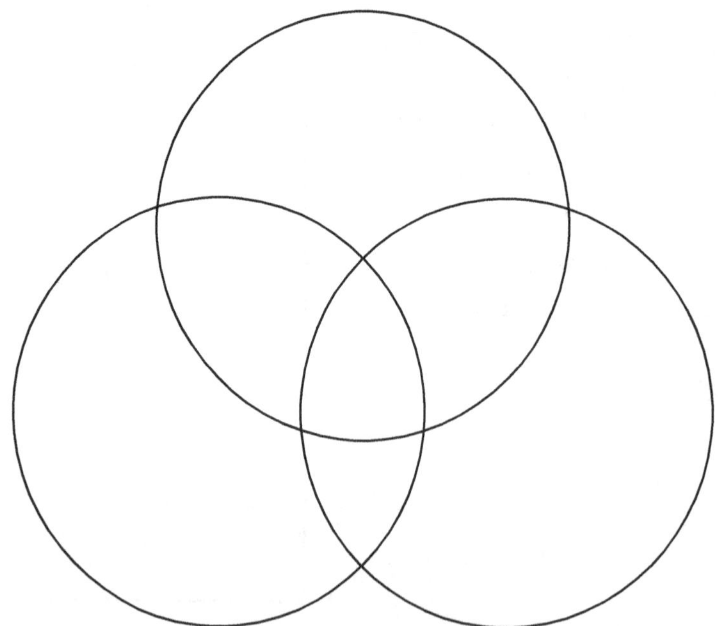

A Trip to New Zealand

What would it be like to travel to New Zealand? How much would it cost? What would you do there? Conduct research and find out.

Directions

1. Suppose you were taking a 6-day/5-night trip to New Zealand. Visit a local travel agent or do research online to find the answers to these questions to help you plan your trip.

   - How much will it cost to fly from your state to New Zealand?

   - How long will it take to get there?

   - How much will it cost to stay in a hotel for 5 nights?

   - How much will it cost to rent a car for 6 days?

   - How much will it cost to eat there?

   - What activities will you choose and how much will they cost?

   - How long will the activities take? (You don't want to miss your flight home!)

2. Fold a sheet of notebook paper into thirds. Then fold the paper in half to make six columns. Label the columns Day 1, Day 2, Day 3, Day 4, Day 5 and Day 6.

3. Figure out your airfare and how long it will take to fly to New Zealand and back home again.

4. Write the information in the Day 1 and Day 6 columns. Plan your rental car, meals, and hotel expenses and record the information in the columns for each day.

5. Fill in the rest of each day with activities and their costs. Don't forget to allow time to sleep! Total the amount in each column. Add the six totals together to figure out the total cost of your trip.

6. Share your trip activities and cost with a group. Listen as they share theirs. Discuss how the trips compare in activities and cost.

> ### Materials:
> New Zealand travel
>   brochures
> New Zealand hotel and
>   flight information
> Internet (optional)
> paper
> pencil

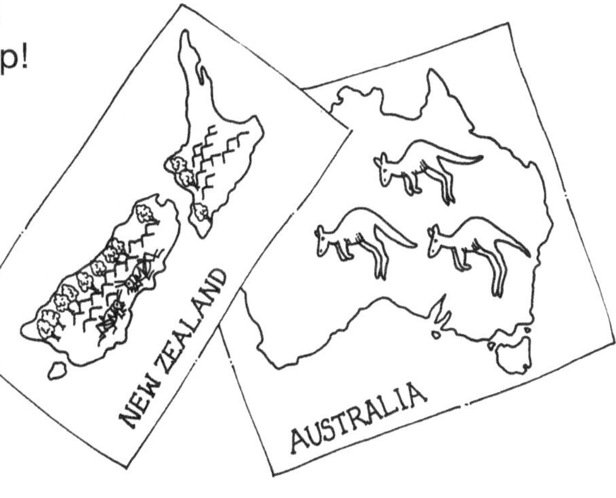

Name That Country

Europe is made up of more than two dozen countries. Play a class game to learn more about where each country is located in relation to others.

Directions

1. Sit outside in a circle with your classmates. Your teacher will write the name of each country on a slip of paper and put it in a jar.

2. Choose a slip of paper from the jar. Find your country on the map below.

3. Make up a clue about your country, such as "I am a small country east of Romania," (Moldova) or "I am the southernmost country in Europe." (Greece)

4. Read your clue when it is your turn. The class has three guesses to answer the question. Try to guess the answers when others say their clues.

Materials:
- jar
- pencil
- paper
- scissors
- quiet outdoor spot

Sing a European Song

There are many songs from Europe that you probably know. Choose one to sing with a group.

Directions

1. As a group, choose a song from a European country. You may choose one from the list below or conduct research to find one of your own. It is best to choose one with a familiar tune.

Materials:

paper
pencil
reference books
Internet (optional)

England
"Here We Go Round the Mulberry Bush"
"London Bridge"

France
"Frére Jacques" (Brother John)
"Au clair de la lune"
(Under the Moonlight)

Scotland
"Zickety Dickety Dock"
(Hickory Dickory Dock)

Germany
"O Tannenbaum" (Oh Christmas Tree)
"Stille Nacht" (Silent Night)

Spain
"Cabeza, Hombros, Piernas, Pies" (Head and Shoulders, Knees and Toes)

2. If the song is in another language, challenge yourself to try and sing it in that language. If not, pronounce the title in the other language and sing the song in English.

3. Perform your song for the class. If you chose your own song, tell the class which country it came from.

4. Summarize what is happening in your song.

Make Tzatziki

Tzatziki is a popular Greek cucumber salad dish that is easy to make. Give it a try!

Directions

1. Combine olive oil, vinegar, garlic, salt, and pepper in a bowl. Mix well and set aside.

2. In another bowl, combine the Greek yogurt and sour cream. Use a whisk to blend well. Add the olive oil mixture to the yogurt mixture and mix well.

3. Finally, add the cucumber and fresh dill. Chill for at least two hours before serving. Eat up!

Materials:

3 tbsp. olive oil
1 tbsp. vinegar
2 tsp. garlic
1/2 tsp. salt
1/4 tsp. white pepper
1 cup Greek yogurt
1 cup sour cream
2 cucumbers, peeled, seeded and diced
1 tsp. chopped fresh dill
mixing bowl
teaspoon
measuring cup
whisk
mixing spoon
bowls and plastic spoons
napkins
*knife and cutting board (unless the cucumbers and dill have already been cut)

Design a Board Game

Learn about many places in Europe by creating a board game with a group.

Directions

1. Work in a group of four. Use a sheet of drawing paper as your board. Draw a path made of squares. Include a "start" square and a "finish" square.

2. Write instructions inside some of the squares, such as "move ahead two spaces," "take another turn," or "ate too much pizza in Italy—lose a turn." Be creative.

3. Use colored pencils or markers to decorate the game board. Then distribute 8 index cards to each person.

4. Use reference books, the map of Europe on page 110, or the Internet to help you write statements and questions, such as "Name a city in Poland," (Warsaw) or "In what country is the Black Forest located?" (Germany). Write the questions on the front of the index card. Write the answers on the back of the index card.

5. Shuffle all of the index cards and set in a stack. Each player will take a card off the top of the stack and try to answer the question. If the player answers the question correctly, he or she will move the game piece marker one square forward. If the player lands on a square with additional instructions, he or she will follow those directions.

6. The first person to reach "finish" wins the game.

Materials:

drawing paper

4 game piece markers

reference books

Internet

32 index cards

colored pencils or markers

Plan a Menu

Are the foods people eat in Russia the same as the foods people eat in Denmark? Do Italy and Ireland grow the same kinds of crops? What kinds of foods do people eat in different regions of Europe? Plan a menu to show your knowledge of food in a European country.

Materials:
- drawing paper
- markers
- reference books
- Internet (optional)

Directions

1. Choose a European country that you would like to visit.

2. Use reference books or the Internet to conduct research to find out what types of foods people like to eat in your chosen country.

3. Fold a sheet of drawing paper into thirds to make your menu.

4. List the dishes by category, such as appetizers, entrées, and desserts.

5. Write a description of each dish and how much it costs.

6. Decorate your menu. Exchange menus with another classmate and order a complete meal for less than twenty dollars.

Famous Places Bingo

**How well do you know famous places in Europe?
Play bingo to find out.**

Mount Vesuvius	The Golden Tower	The Louvre
Old Rauma	The Acropolis	Stonehenge
Red Square	Jungfrau	Loch Ness
Grand Place	Marko's Fortress	Myvatn

Materials:
12 index cards
27 playing markers
   (or pennies)
pencils
reference books
Internet (optional)

Directions

1. Form groups of four. Each group member will

   a) choose three famous places listed in the box and write the names at the bottom of the blank side of the index cards. Each place should be written down only once.

   b) use the Internet or reference books to find out what the famous place looks like and where it is located.

   c) draw a picture of the place on the blank side of the index card above the name. On the other side, write the name of the country where the famous place is located.

2. As a group, spend 2-3 minutes reading all of the famous places and their locations.

3. Each group member will make a bingo card with nine squares (three rows of three). In each square, write down the names of the countries where the famous places are located. Each bingo card should have nine different countries listed.

4. Choose one member of the group to be the bingo caller. Then, distribute nine playing markers or pennies to each of the other three players.

5. The bingo caller will shuffle the twelve index cards, call out the name of the famous place, and show the other players the drawing of the famous place.

6. As each famous place is named, each player will cover the name of the corresponding country if it appears on the bingo card. Call out "Bingo" if you are the first to cover three countries in a row, a column, or a diagonal line.

7. Check answers by flipping over the cards that have been read aloud. Repeat the game until every member of the group has had a chance to be the bingo caller.

Multiple Intelligences G4–6, SV 9780547625744

Play German Games

German children play games that you may be familiar with, too. Some of these games include the following:

Verstecken (hide and seek)
Fangen (tag)
Hüpfspiele (hopscotch)

Directions

1. Use a German-English dictionary or the Internet to look up each of these German words: ***verstecken***, ***fangen***, ***hupfen***, and ***spielen***. Discuss what each word means and why the games have these names.

2. Go outside and form three groups. Each group will play a different German game. Say the name of each game as you play.

3. Group 1 plays Verstecken.

4. Group 2 plays Fangen.

5. Group 3 plays Hüpfspiele. Before playing, draw hopscotch squares on the pavement with chalk. If playing on a dirt surface, use a stick to draw the squares. Take turns tossing the stone and playing. Remember not to hop in the square where the stone lands!

6. Rotate until everyone has played all of the games.

7. Sit in a class circle and take turns telling which game is your favorite.

> **Materials:**
> large outdoor spot
> chalk or stick
> stone
> German-English dictionary
> Internet (optional)

Write a Pen Pal Letter

How is a typical day for you similar to a typical day for a student who lives in Europe? How is it different? Write a pen pal letter and find out.

Directions

1. Choose a country in Europe. Write a letter to a fictional student who lives in that country.

2. Tell about a typical day in your life (school, homework, hobbies, and so on).

3. Then ask questions about a typical day in your pen pal's life.

4. Seal your letter in an envelope and switch letters with a partner.

5. Use reference books or the Internet to answer your partner's questions.

6. Write back to your partner and seal the letter in the other envelope. Switch letters and read your pen pal's response.

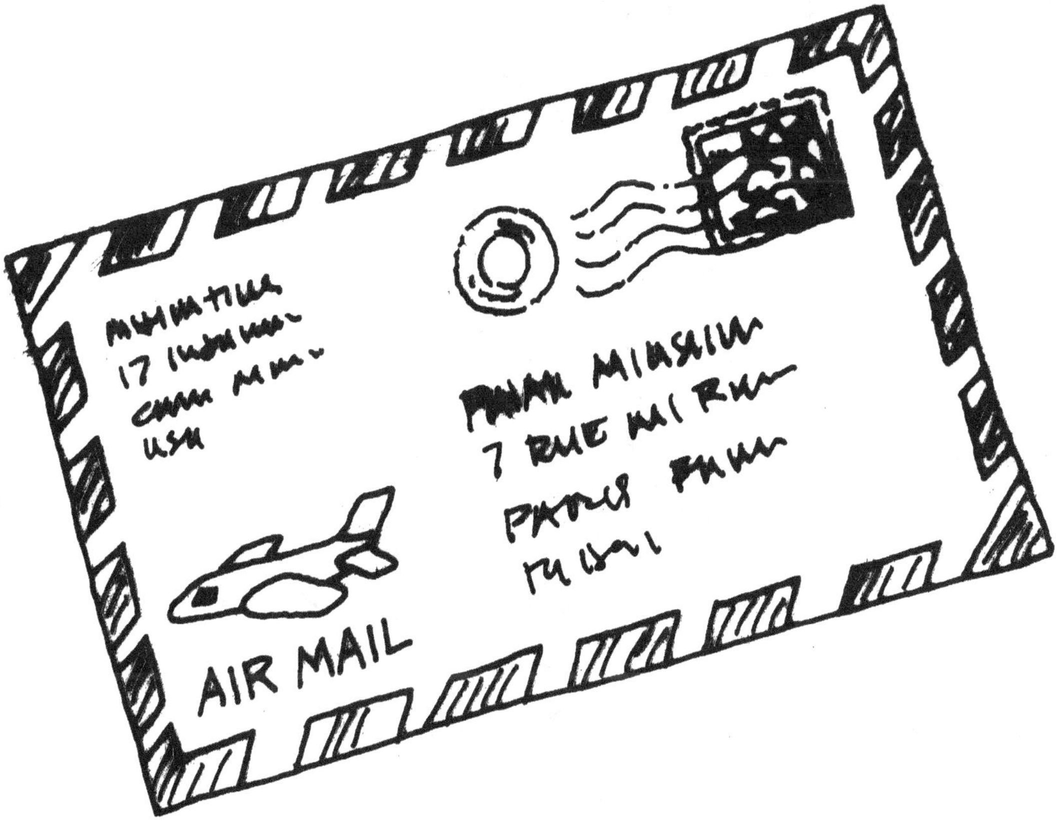

Materials:

paper
pencil
2 envelopes
reference books
Internet (optional)

Multiple Intelligences G4–6, SV 9780547625744

Name _______________________________   Date _______________

Make a Picture Dictionary

Make a picture dictionary to help you learn to speak different European languages!

Directions

1. Fold a sheet of construction paper in half to make the cover of your picture dictionary.

2. Fold several sheets of blank paper in half and insert them inside of the cover. Staple the pages and the cover together.

3. Alphabetize and write down the names of simple nouns in English.

4. Leave space after each noun so you can draw a picture of it.

5. Use reference books or the Internet to find out the meaning of each word in one or more European languages. Write the name of the language in parentheses following the word.

6. Page through your picture dictionary to recall the European names. Then trade dictionaries with a partner and try to learn some of his or her words.

Materials:

construction paper
pencil
blank paper
reference books
Internet (optional)
stapler

cat

gato (Spanish)

chat (French)

katze (German)

72

Analyze a Cartogram

A cartogram is a map in which the size and shape of
the land changes based on the data it is measuring.
It often uses circles or rectangles to display data.
Suppose a cartogram shows the area of forest
land in Country A and Country B. On a traditional
map, Country A and Country B are the same size.
However, if Country A has twice as much forest land
as Country B, the cartogram will show Country A two
times larger in size. Look at the cartogram of Asia below.

Materials:
map of Asia
ruler
pencil or pen

Directions

1. Answer the questions based on the cartogram below:

   Which country is larger—Bangladesh or Bhutan? _______________________

   About how much larger—2 times, 10 times, 100 times? _______________________

2. Answer the questions based on a map of Asia (see page 112):

   Which country is larger—Bangladesh or Bhutan? _______________________

   About how much larger—2 times, 10 times, 100 times? _______________________

3. Based on the information above, does the cartogram measure population size or
   land size? Explain.

   ____

4. Use a ruler to measure the area of two
   countries shown on the cartogram.
   Compare the data. Now look at the
   same two countries on the map.
   What conclusions can you draw?

   ____

   ____

   ____

   ____

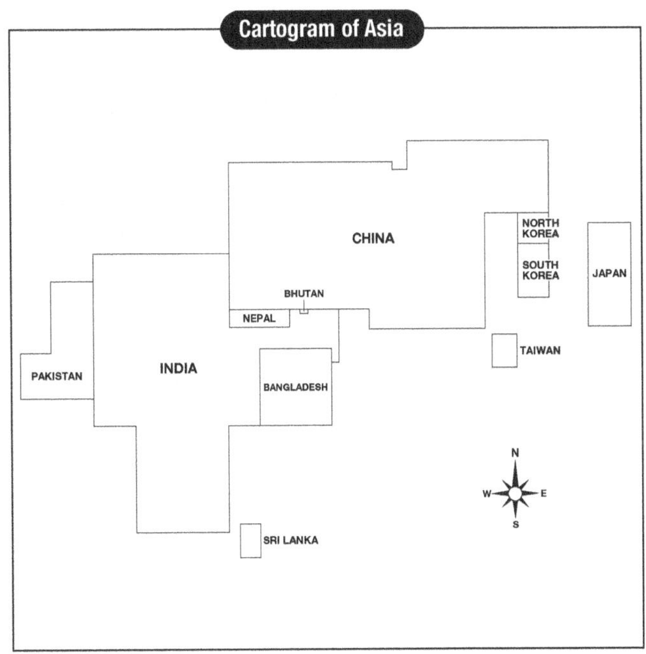

Multiple Intelligences G4–6, SV 9780547625744

Unit 9: Asia

Write a Haiku

A haiku is a Japanese poem usually written about nature. A haiku has three unrhymed lines of five, seven, and five syllables. Write a haiku about nature.

Materials:
paper
pencil
a quiet outdoor spot

Directions

1. Find a quiet spot outside. Sit down and read the haiku below. Clap out the syllables and count out the 5-7-5 pattern.

2. Look and listen to the sights and sounds around you. What do you see?

3. Close your eyes. What do you hear? What do you picture in your mind?

4. Use your reflections to write a haiku. Clap and count until you have formed a 5-7-5 pattern. See example below.

5. Illustrate your haiku. Find a partner and take turns reading your haikus.

Daffodils spring up

from yesterday's frozen ground.

They reach to the sky.

Make Date Macaroons

Dates are a food that is native to the Middle East. During the fast of Ramadan, Muslims break their fast each evening by eating a few dates and drinking a glass of water. You can make date macaroons to eat with your classmates.

Directions

1. Preheat oven to 325 degrees.

2. Soak the pitted dates in water to soften. Drain and pat dry before use.

3. Place the pitted dates, banana, and coconut flakes in a food processor. Process until smooth and moist. If dough is too gooey, add more coconut flakes.

4. Place rounded tablespoons of dough on cookie sheet, about an inch apart.

5. Bake at 325 degrees for 10-15 minutes. Cool and serve.

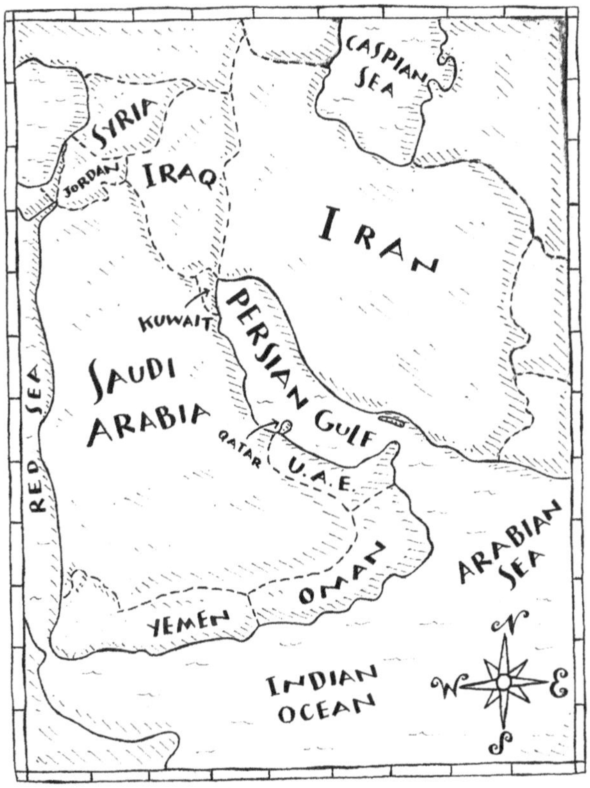

Materials:

8 medium dates, pitted

1 banana

1 ½ cups of coconut flakes

food processor

tablespoon

baking sheet

use of an oven

Dates are native to the Middle East.

What Animal Are You?

The Chinese zodiac follows a 13-year cycle. Each year is represented by a different animal. Each animal has different strengths and weaknesses. Are you a dog, dragon, horse, monkey, ox, pig, rabbit, rat, rooster, sheep, snake, or tiger?

Directions

1. Cut out the Chinese zodiac wheel below. Glue the wheel to a sheet of construction paper and cut it out.

2. Place the wheel in the center of an 8 x 10 piece of poster board. Push a paper fastener through both the wheel and the poster board. Adjust the paper fastener so that it is not too tight or too loose. (The wheel should spin freely.)

3. Draw a down arrow at the top of the wheel. Spin the wheel until the arrow is pointing down at the year you were born. What animal are you?

4. Use reference books or the Internet to find out about the character traits that describe your animal. Do these traits describe you?

5. Draw pictures and write down the traits on the poster board. Use your Chinese zodiac wheel to find the animals that represent each person in your family.

Materials:

construction paper
paper fastener
scissors
poster board
glue stick
markers
pencil
reference books
Internet (optional)

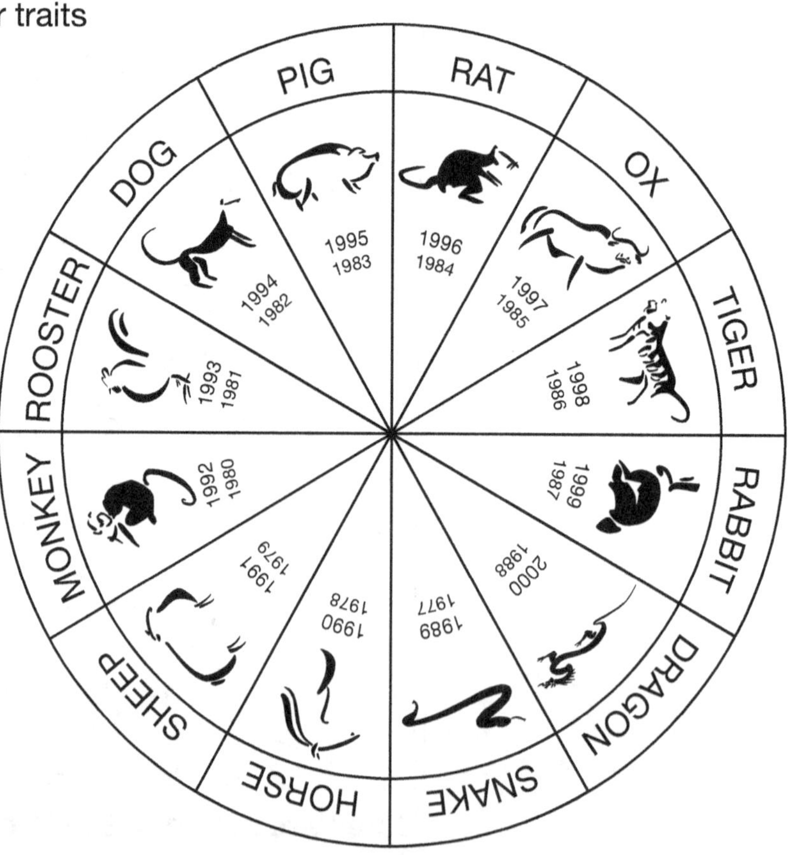

Multiple Intelligences G4–6, SV 9780547625744

Write a Chant

Write a chant with your group to teach others about a country in Asia. Then have fun performing your chant.

Directions

1. With your group members, choose a country in Asia. Use reference books or the Internet to conduct research to find out about its location, cities, culture, geography, or history.

2. Use the information you found to write a chant. See the two examples below.

   Sri Lanka is south of India.
   It is close to the Arabian Sea.
   The capital city is Colombo.
   Pack your bags and go.

   or

   Malaysia, Malaysia,
   of Southeast Asia,
   pretty beaches
   but jungle leeches!

3. Chant the words with your group. Clap your hands or tap your foot to the rhythm.

4. Practice your chant and use gestures to act it out. Then go outside to perform for your class!

> **Materials:**
> paper
> pencil
> outdoor spot
>   (for performing)
> reference books
> Internet (optional)

Make a Historical Map

Historical maps display information from a particular time period in the past. For this reason, historical maps of a region can look very different from a modern-day map of the same region. Compare a historical map with a present-day map.

<table>
<tr><td>

Directions

1 Use a copy of the Eastern Hemisphere map from page 113.

2. Study the map of Kublai Khan's empire and Marco Polo's routes below. Then, use a pencil to lightly draw Marco Polo's routes on your copy of the Eastern Hemisphere map that shows the current country borders.

</td><td>

Materials:

drawing paper

pencil

map of Eastern
   Hemisphere

yarn (2 different colors)

scissors

tape

</td></tr>
</table>

3. Cut a piece of yarn long enough to cover the route to China and within China. Secure the yarn to the route with tape.

4. Cut a piece of yarn of a different color. Tape the yarn along Marco Polo's return route.

5. Discuss Marco Polo's routes and the cities and countries he would pass through today. Estimate the number of miles he traveled to China, within China, and back home again.

Research an Asian Culture

Asia is a continent made up of diverse countries, people, and customs. Countries celebrate their cultures in many different ways. Research an Asian country to find out about its special culture.

Directions

1. Choose a country you would like to research. Make a web like the one shown below. Write the name of the country in the center. Leave room to draw pictures.

2. Use reference books or the Internet to find out more about the country's culture. Research and write facts in 8 circles like the ones shown below. Include information about religion, holidays, food, clothing, dance, traditions, theater, and art.

3. Use the information to draw a picture in the center that highlights some of the information you found. Present your country's culture to the class.

Materials:
pencil
paper
reference books
Internet (optional)
drawing paper
colored pencils

Outdoor Reader's Theater

Present a reader's theater skit to tell what your group knows about countries in Asia.

Directions

1. Sit outside with group members. Brainstorm a list of all the things you know about the countries that make up Asia.

2. Choose one or two ideas for your skit. Decide what the characters will say and do. Decide how the characters will convey the information. Make sure every group member has a part.

3. Write down what the characters will say and practice reading the parts.

4. Speak with expression and use gestures to make your character interesting.

5. Perform your skit for the class.

Materials:

paper
pencil
quiet outdoor spot

Draw a Manga Comic Strip

Manga is a popular form of Japanese animation, or anime. Create your own manga characters for an anime comic strip.

Materials:
drawing paper
pencils
colored pencils

Directions

1. Fold a sheet of drawing paper to make 6 squares (2 rows of 3 squares) Decide on a simple story or dialogue that can be told in six frames.

2. Look at the four manga faces below to learn how to draw anime style. Lightly draw a circle and divide it into fourths. Use these proportions to draw the face.

3. Notice that some faces are round, while others are angular. Younger characters usually have rounder faces. Older characters usually have angular faces.

4. Anime characters have very large eyes. They should be drawn on or above the horizontal line.

5. The nose and mouth should be drawn about halfway between the horizontal line and the bottom edge of the circle. Experiment to see what you like best.

6. Draw your comic strip and use speech bubbles to show dialogue. Color your comic strip and present it to the class.

Build an African Zoo

Many animals are native to Africa. Research one and form a class zoo.

Directions

1. Use reference books or the Internet to research an African animal from the list below. Jot down facts on a sheet of paper, including the animal's habitat, food sources, and other interesting facts.

aardvark	lemur	jackal
African lion	warthog	rhinoceros
wildebeest	ostrich	mamba
hyena	crocodile	Colobus monkey
eland	okapi	gecko
fossa	giraffe	hare
kudu	grysbok	zebra
baboon	water buffalo	hippopotamus

2. Fold a 4 x 12 piece of poster board in half so it will stand up like a card on a table.

3. On the front of the card, draw and color a picture of your animal and write its name underneath the drawing.

4. Use your facts to write a paragraph about your animal inside of the card.

5. As a class, decide how to classify the animals into groups. Set up the groups in different areas of the zoo. Place your zoo animal with the zoo animals in its group.

6. Walk around the zoo and read about the different African animals.

7. Tell a partner three new things that you learned.

Play a Logic Game

Africa is made up of many countries. Can you guess which one your partner has chosen?

Directions

1. Use a map of Africa to write in the names of the African countries on the map below. Then find a partner to play a logic game.

2. Choose a country and write the name of it on the back of your paper. Do not show your partner what you have written. Your partner will do the same.

3. Take turns asking a yes or no question, such as "Is your country in Central Africa?" or "Is your country west of Chad?"

4. Lightly draw a small X in each country that does not answer the question. For example:

   - If your partner's country is located in Central Africa, draw X's in the countries that are NOT part of Central Africa.

   - If your partner's country is NOT located in Central Africa, draw X's in the countries that are part of Central Africa.

5. The first person to guess the other's country wins the game. Erase the X's and play again.

Materials:
pencil
map of Africa

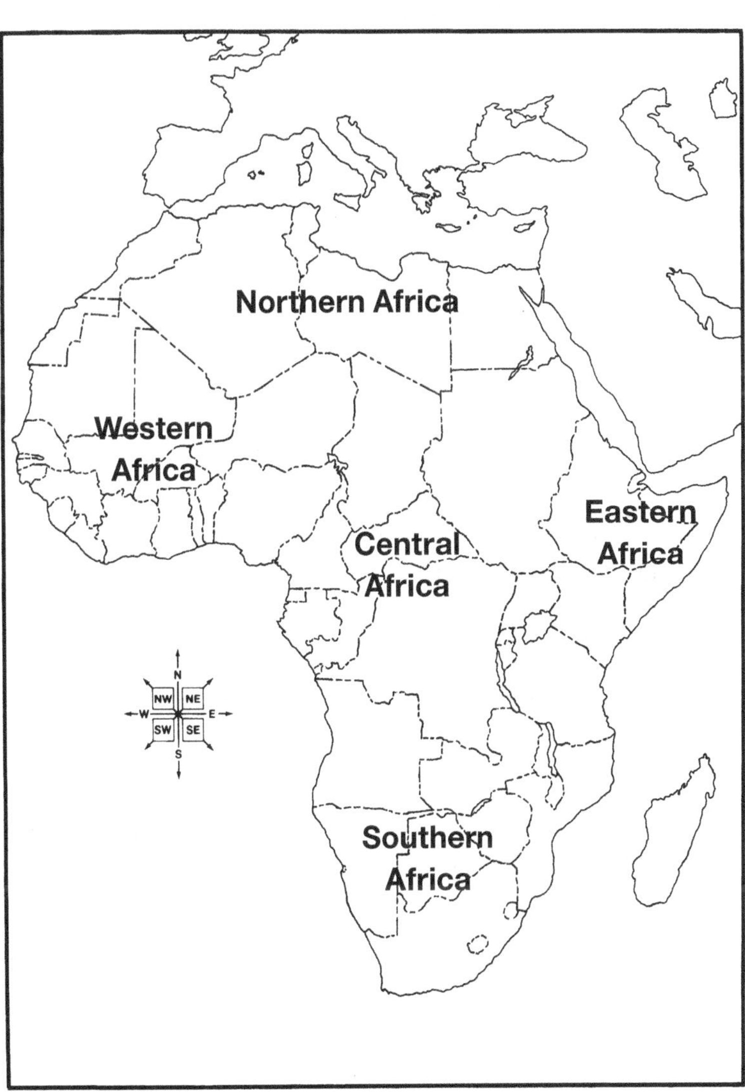

Write an African Tale

Many folktales are porquoi stories. A porquoi story is a fictional tale that explains why something is the way it is. Read the South African porquoi tale below and then write one of your own.

Directions

Read the South African folktale below. Then write your own to explain why something is the way it is. When you are finished, read your story to the class.

Cloud Eating
A South African folktale

One day Jackal and Hyena were playing together when they saw a white cloud rise into the sky. Jackal jumped on the cloud and began to eat it as though it were made of fat.

As Jackal was eating, the cloud continued to rise higher into the sky, and Jackal was afraid to jump down. He said to Hyena, "My friend, I will save half of this cloud for you if you catch me when I jump." So Hyena caught Jackal and broke his fall. Then she leaped into the sky to eat her portion of the cloud.

When she was done, she called out to Jackal, "My dear friend, now catch me when I jump."

The Jackal replied, "Jump down when you are ready. I will catch you."

Jackal lifted up his arms, and Hyena jumped down from the cloud. But, before Hyena reached the ground, Jackal cried out in pain, dropped his arms, and jumped to the side. Hyena hit the ground hard and was hurt.

"Dear friend, I am sorry. Please do not be angry. I stepped on a thorn and jumped in pain before I could catch you."

Since that day, Hyena's hind feet have been shorter and smaller than the front ones.

Multiple Intelligences G4–6, SV 9780547625744

Write an African Praise Song

An African praise song is one of the most common forms of poetry in Africa. Each line of the song includes a praise name, similar to a nickname, that describes a person's traits, emotions, or actions. Praise songs are part of a long oral tradition and often include information about a person's family or clan.

```
Materials: ______________
paper
pencil
```

Directions

1. Decide whether you want to write a praise song about yourself or about someone that you admire.

2. Use the structure outlined below to write a praise song about yourself or someone you admire. If you wish you may continue the poem with more praise names or descriptions. An example has been provided.

Praise Song Structure	**Example**
Name of the person	She is Tori
Name of parent	Daughter of Paul
Praise name and/or description	Running tiger who chases away trouble
Name of other parent	Daughter of Rose
Praise name and/or description	Graceful guard protecting all she loves

3. As you write, remember that you will be reading or chanting your poem aloud. Be sure to pay attention to the rhythm of the lines.

4. Practice performing your poem. Add gestures and movements to add interest. Then, read it aloud to the class.

Create a Mask for the Festival of Masks

The Festival of Masks is one of the Ivory Coast's most famous festivals. Small villages hold contests to reveal the best dancers. The dancers perform while wearing intricately designed masks. Make your own mask for the Festival of Masks.

Directions

1. Create a symmetrical mask like the ones shown below. Draw an outline of your mask on a sheet of cardboard.

2. Cut out your mask. Hold the mask up to your face and mark the two places for eyeholes.

3. Cut out the eyeholes and look through the mask. Make sure they are large enough for you to see clearly.

4. Draw designs on your mask and then paint it.

5. When dry, glue on yarn, beads, straw, pebbles, and other decorations.

6. When your mask is completely finished, punch a hole in each side.

7. Thread and fasten two pieces of yarn through the holes. Tie on your mask and prepare to dance outdoors in the Festival of Masks.

Materials:

- cardboard
- pencil
- paint
- paintbrush
- jar of water (for rinsing brush)
- hole punch
- yarn
- beads, pebbles, straw, and other decorations
- large outdoor area

Multiple Intelligences G4–6, SV 9780547625744

Construct a Pyramid Bedroom

Pharaohs had their workers build huge pyramids. The ancient Egyptians believed in an afterlife and the pharaohs wanted to take their belongings with them. Each pyramid held the pharaoh's tomb and his treasures. Scientists study the artifacts inside of the ancient pyramids to learn more about ancient Egyptian culture. What belongings would you want to include in your pyramid?

Directions

1. On a piece of poster board, design a pattern for a square pyramid as shown on the right.

2. Measure carefully so that the sides are congruent. Check your accuracy by folding the pattern. Correct any mistakes.

3. Unfold the pattern and lay it flat on your desk. Draw the floor of your bedroom (bed, rug, etc.) on the base of the pyramid. Draw pictures of the items you'd like to have in your pyramid on the sides.

4. Decorate the outside of your pyramid. Fold up three sides and tape them together. Leave the fourth side down so others can peek into your bedroom pyramid.

5. On a separate sheet of paper, write a brief paragraph explaining why you chose the items that you did.

Materials:

poster board

paper

pencil

scissors

tape

ruler

markers

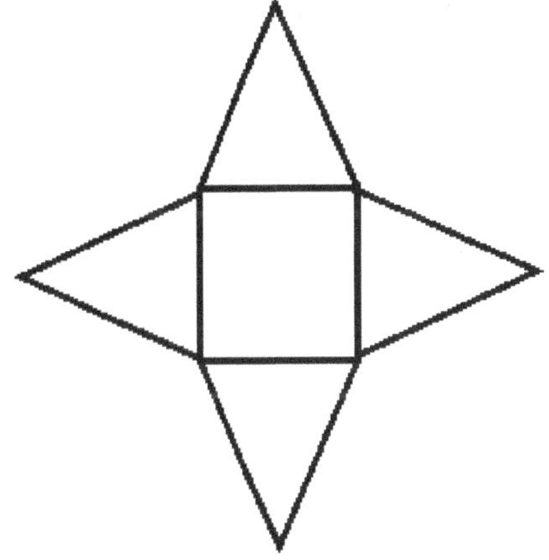

Play Mamba

A mamba is a huge, poisonous South African snake. It is also the name of a game that African children play. Play a game of Mamba with your classmates.

Materials:

a large outdoor area

Directions

1. Mark off a large area for the game. Choose one person to be the mamba.

2. When the game begins, keep away from the mamba without going outside of the marked off area.

3. The mamba tries to catch the players. When players are caught, they become part of the mamba's body by placing their hands on the shoulders or waist of the person in front of them.

4. Only the mamba's head (the person who was chosen at the beginning of the game) can catch new players. The mamba uses its body (the captured players) to catch other players.

5. Players cannot run between the mamba's body and its head. The winner is the last person remaining. He or she becomes the new mamba.

Multiple Intelligences G4–6, SV 9780547625744

Make and Play a Mancala Game

Mancala is a popular game played in Africa. Make your own mancala game and play against a partner.

<table>
<tr><td>

Materials:

1 egg carton

2 cups

2 sets of 24 playing markers

outdoor spot

</td></tr>
</table>

Directions

1. Cut off the top of an empty egg carton to make a mancala board. Take the egg carton, playing markers, and 2 cups outside. The object of the game is to capture as many markers as you can and place them in your empty cup (mancala cup).

2. Sit across from your partner. Your playing side is the row of 6 holes closest to you. Place the 2 mancala cups on either side of the egg carton. The cup on the right is yours and the cup on the left is your partner's.

3. Each player takes 24 markers and puts 4 markers in each of his or her 6 holes. To play, pick up 4 markers from one of your holes.

4. Go counterclockwise and place one marker in each hole along the way. (Never put a marker in your partner's mancala cup.)

5. Take turns picking up markers from your holes and distributing one in each hole counterclockwise. (As the game continues, some holes might be filled with both you and your partner's markers; others might be completely empty.)

6. If you place your last marker in an empty hole on your side of the board, take all of your partner's markers from his or her hole directly across from your empty hole. Place the captured markers in your mancala cup.

7. The game ends when one player is out of markers on his or her side of the board. Count the markers in the mancala cups. The player with the most markers wins the game.

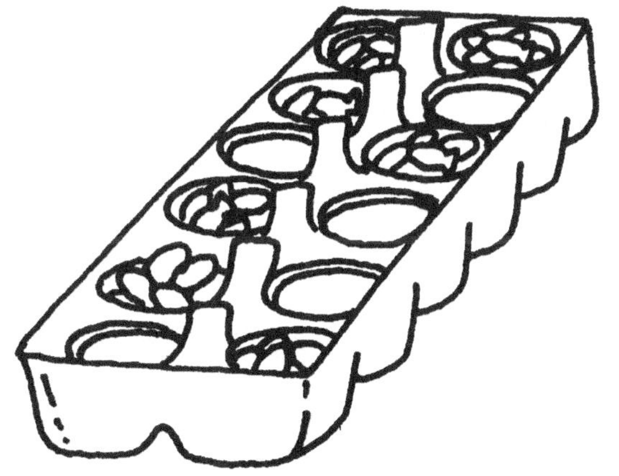

Weather in Africa

**Africa is divided into eight climatic zones:
Tropical Wet, Tropical Wet-Dry, Steppe, Desert,
Mediterranean, Subtropic Humid, and Highlands.
What is the weather like in each of these zones?**

Directions

1. Form groups of four. Review the map of climatic
   zones in Africa and the map of African countries.

2. Give each group member four index cards. On two of the index cards, write the
   name of two different climatic zones. On the other two index cards, write the name
   of two different African countries. (Do not repeat any climatic zones or countries.)

3. Set aside the index cards with the country names.

4. Use reference books or the Internet to research two climatic zones. Write a brief
   description of the climates on the back of the corresponding climatic zone index
   cards.

5. As a group, study the climate map and review the different types of weather typical
   to each zone.

6. Shuffle the cards with the country names and have one group member choose a
   card and read the name of the country. See who can correctly name the climatic
   zone(s) of the country the fastest.

Materials:

16 index cards

pencils

reference books

Internet (optional)

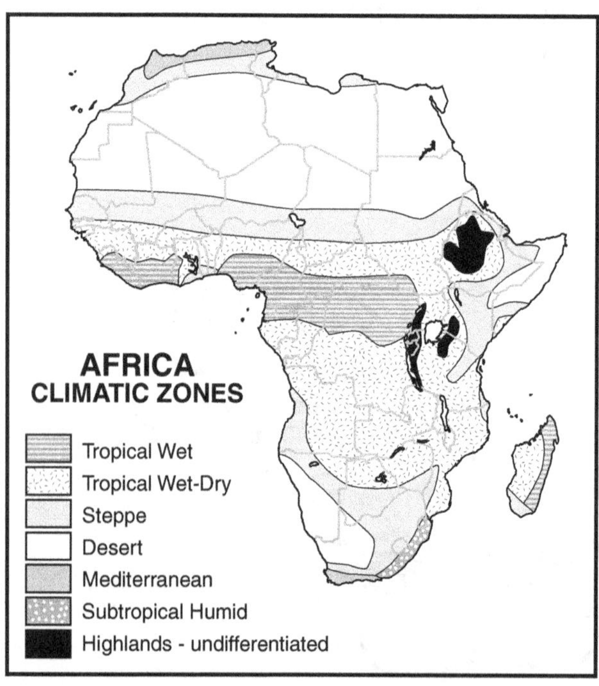

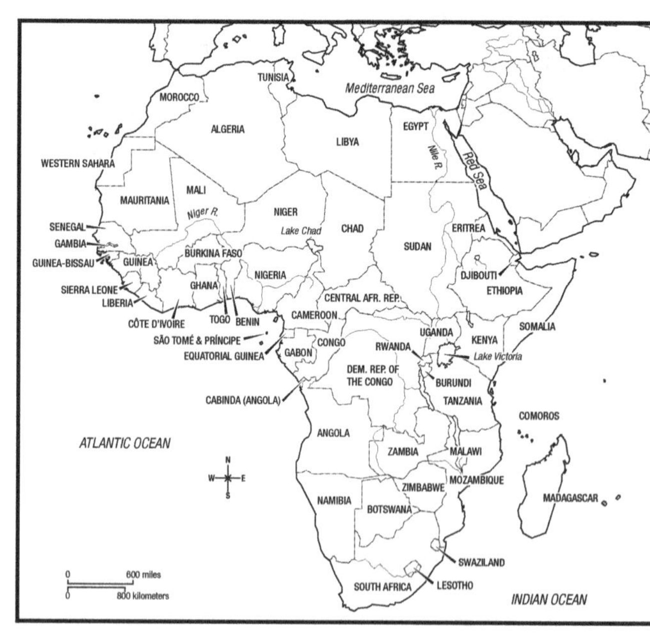

Working at a Maquiladora

A maquiladora is an assembly line plant in Mexico, usually located along the border between the United States and Mexico. The United States ships parts and materials to the maquiladora. Workers assemble the product and then ship the finished products back to the United States. Work with a group to produce shirts at a maquiladora.

Directions

1. Work in groups of four. Distribute a shirt pattern, pair of scissors, a pencil, two sheets of paper, and a penny to each of the group members. Place the other materials in the center of the table.

2. Explain that each member will work individually to create a shirt by following the steps below. Review the steps with the group before continuing.

3. Use a stopwatch to time how long it takes for the group to create the shirts individually. Begin the time and instruct the group to begin.

   Step 1) Use the shirt pattern to trace and cut out two shirts.

   Step 2) Draw stripes and two pockets on each shirt as shown.

   Step 3) Trace a penny on construction paper and cut out the circles to make buttons.

   Step 4) Glue the buttons down the center of the shirt.

4. When all members have finished, stop the time and write down how long it took the group to finish.

5. Now work as an assembly line. Assign each member one step to complete. The first person on the assembly line will trace and cut out eight shirts. As each member finishes the task for one shirt, pass the paper to the next person to complete the next step.

6. Start the time and work until all shirts are completed. Stop the time and write down how long it took the group to finish. Compare and discuss what happened in the two methods of creating a shirt.

Materials:

16 sheets of paper

4 shirt patterns

colored pencils

4 pairs of scissors

construction paper

4 pennies

glue

stopwatch

Charting Longitude and Latitude

What countries come to mind when you think of
North America—Canada, the United States, and
Mexico? Well, there are many more. Use longitude
and latitude to find out where they are located.

Materials:
____
map or globe
(longitude and latitude)

Directions

1. Use a map or globe to draw and label the lines of longitude
   and latitude on the map below.

2. Find a partner. Call out a pair of longitude and latitude coordinates.
   Let your partner find them on the map and tell you which country
   is closest to the location. Switch roles.

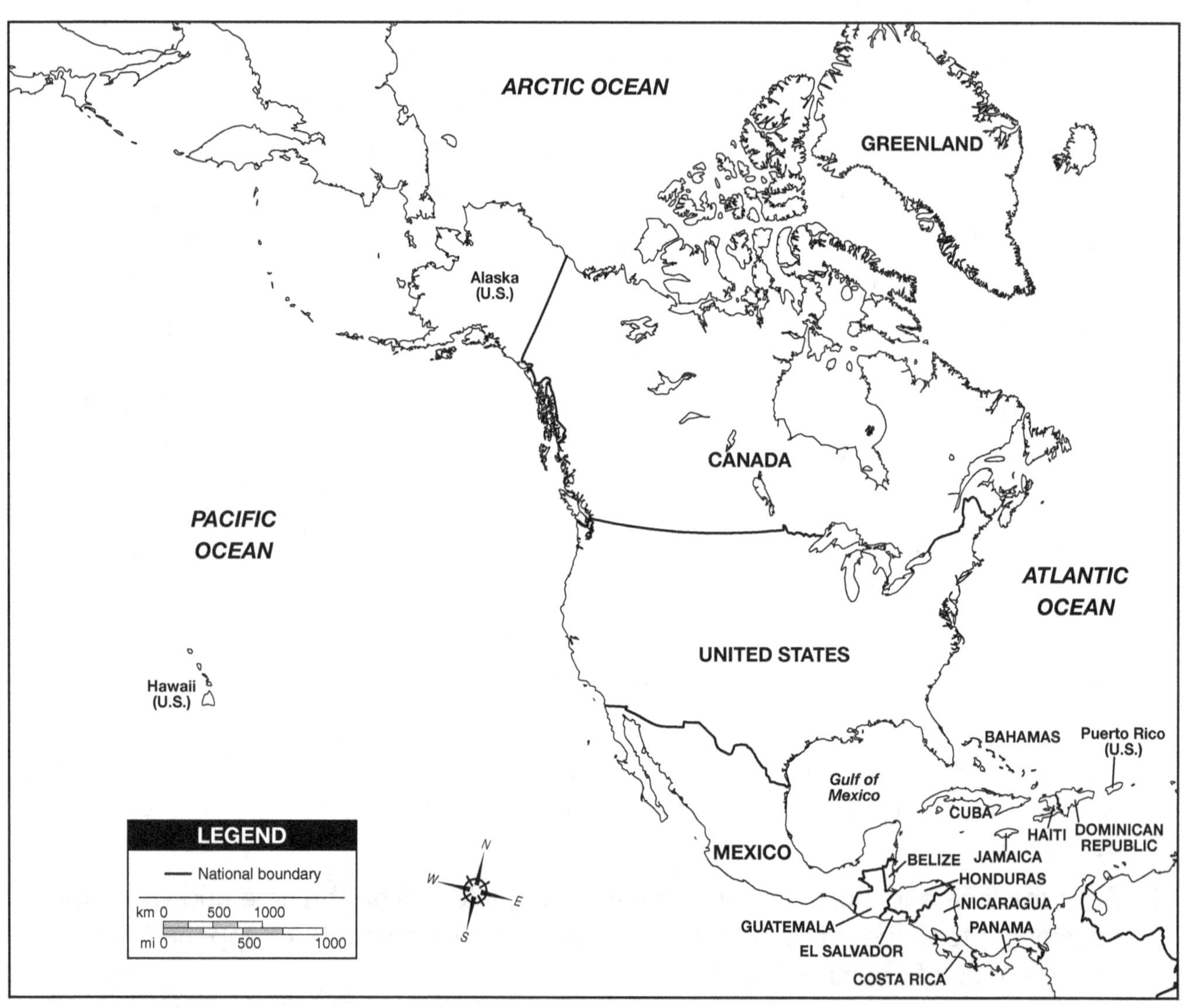

Multiple Intelligences G4–6, SV 9780547625744

Sail on an Alaskan Cruise

Imagine what it would be like to take a cruise along the Alaskan coast. Keep a journal of your ports of call, or the places where the ship stops and tourists can get off of the boat.

Materials:

reference books
Internet (optional)
map of Alaska

Directions

1. Below is the itinerary for your trip:
   Prince Rupert (Canada); Ketchickan; Sitka; Juneau;
   Skagway; Valdez; Anchorage

2. Find each location on a map of Alaska and label it on the map below. Draw lines to connect the seven ports of call. This is the cruise route.

3. Use reference books or the Internet to research the seven ports of call.

4. Use the information to write a short journal entry about each of the seven places. Include information about the weather, landforms, and special things to do in the city.

5. Share your journal entries with a partner. Tell about your favorite port of call and what makes it so special.

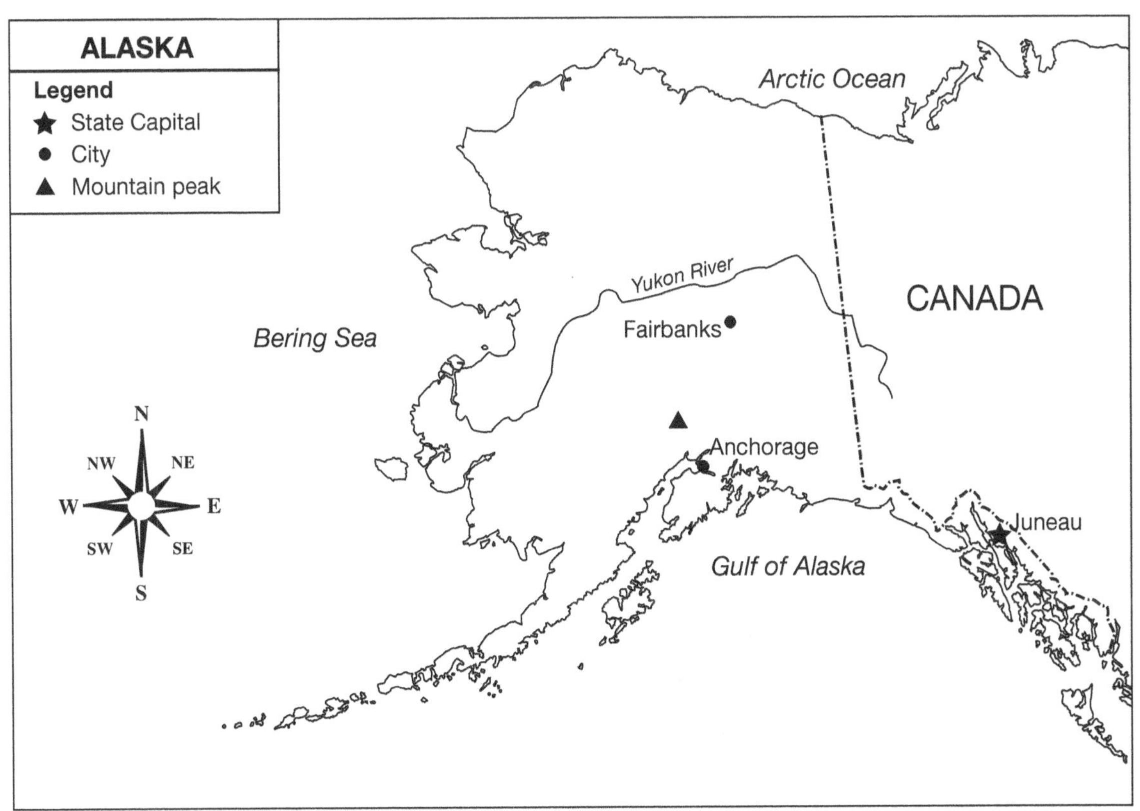

Write a Capital Song

Look at the map of Central America below. Can you name all of the capitals?

Directions

1. Use reference books, the Internet, or a map of Central America to locate the capital cities of the countries labeled on the map of Central America below. Then label them on the map below. Take turns trying to name the nine capital cities.

2. Work with a group to write a song to help you remember the names of the capitals. Practice the song and then perform it for the class.

3. Again, take turns trying to name the capital cities. Discuss how the song helped you retain the information.

Materials: _______________

reference books

Internet (optional)

pencil

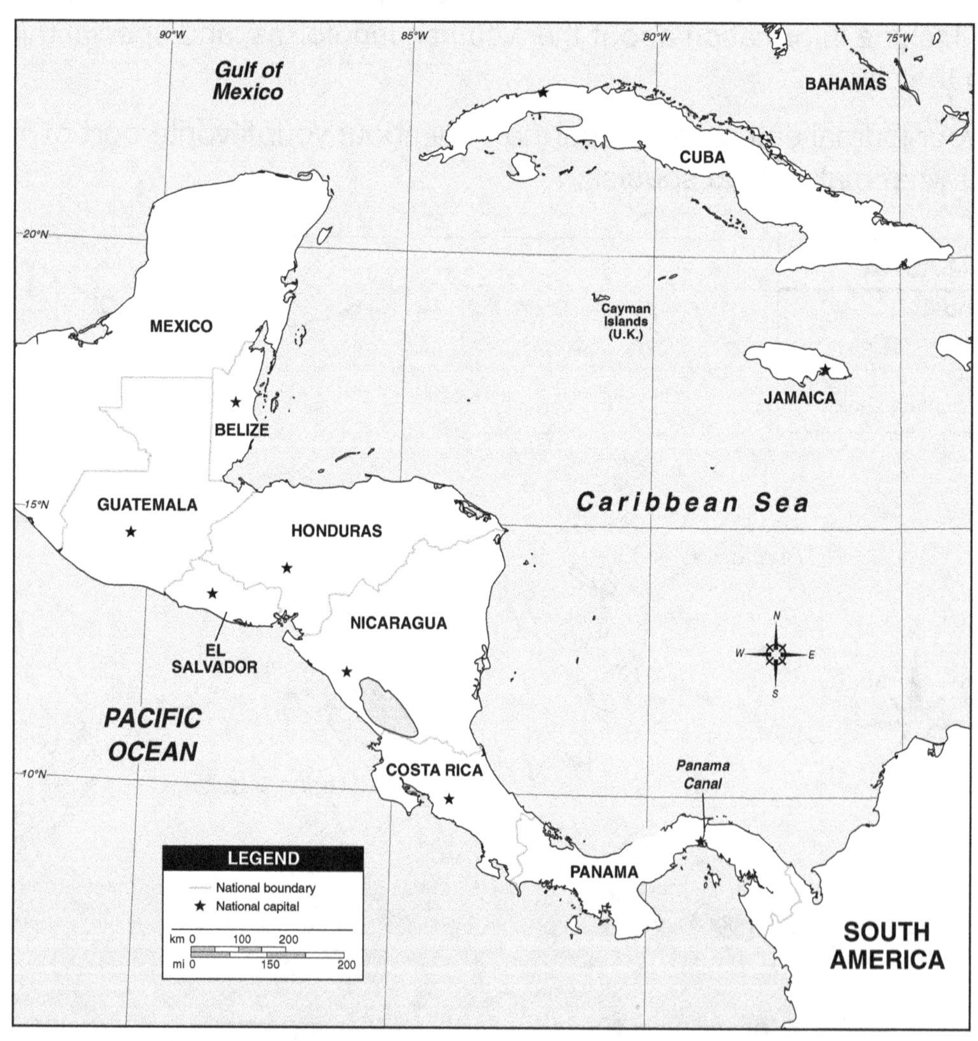

Multiple Intelligences G4–6, SV 9780547625744

Design a Viking Ship

The Viking people settled in Greenland more than one thousand years ago. About 80% of Greenland is covered by sheets of ice, so travel by water was essential. The Vikings built far more advanced ships than those built in other countries. Work with a group to reproduce the design of a Viking ship.

Materials:
reference books
Internet (optional)
poster board
pencil

Directions

1. Work with a group to draw a design of a Viking ship. Use reference books or the Internet to conduct research to find out the differences between the drekar and the knarr—two types of Viking longships.

2. Choose either the drekar or the knarr and reproduce its design on a sheet of poster board.

3. Label the ship's parts, such as the keel, hull, crossbeams, and so on. Write about the parts and their purposes.

4. Present your reproduction to the class and explain how Viking longships helped the Vikings survive in their environment.

Central American Dances

Dancing is an important part of Central American culture. Find out about Central American dances and how their styles are different.

Directions

1. If your teacher plays music, listen to the different types of Central American music. Then work with a group to choose five dance styles to research from the box below.

<table>
<tr><td>rumba</td><td>samba</td><td>salsa</td><td>mambo</td><td>merengue</td></tr>
<tr><td>cha-cha</td><td>bachata</td><td>bomba</td><td>cumbia</td><td>tango</td></tr>
</table>

Materials:

reference books
Internet (optional)
paper
pencil
Central American music (if possible)

2. Use reference books or the Internet to research the dance styles. Make a chart to record information from your research. Make columns as follows:

   type of dance
   country of origin
   beats per measure
   step pattern (quick and slow beats)

3. Share your chart with the class. If possible, present a few basic steps of a dance from your chart.

Multiple Intelligences G4–6, SV 9780547625744

Measure the Pan-American Highway

The Pan-American Highway is one of the longest highways in the world. It links North America and South America. The North American section of the Pan-American Highway begins in Prudhoe Bay, Alaska, and ends in Yaviza, Panama. How many miles long is the North American route?

Materials:

map of North America

Directions

Look at the map below of the Pan-American Highway. Use a map of North America to calculate the number of miles between cities. Add the distances up to find the total number of miles. Measure both the route passing through Dallas, Texas, and the one passing through Albuquerque, New Mexico. How many miles is each? Compare your answers with others.

North American Route of Pan-American Highway

Multiple Intelligences G4–6, SV 9780547625744

Make Guacamole

**Guacamole is a traditional food eaten in Mexico.
Make guacamole with a group.**

Directions

1. Peel both avocados and remove the pits.

2. Peel and chop the onion and the garlic. Then chop the tomato.

3. Mash the avocado in a bowl and then stir in the remaining ingredients.

4. Serve cold with tortillas and enjoy!

Materials:

2 ripe avocados
½ small onion
1 clove garlic
1 small tomato
juice from a fresh lime
salt and pepper to taste
2 large bowls (guacamole; chips)
knife
spoon
cutting board
styrofoam or paper plates

A Man, a Plan, a Canal: Panama

The Panama Canal is modern engineering feat that connects the Atlantic and Pacific Oceans. Use the palindrome *A Man, a Plan, a Canal: Panama* to help you remember facts about this famous canal.

Directions

Use reference books or the Internet to research the Panama Canal. Use the palindrome to help focus your research.

- A man: Who was the chief engineer who saw the canal to completion?

- A plan: How do the locks work?

- A canal: How did the canal affect world commerce? What were the benefits of using the canal? How much time and distance did it save?

- Panama: Who controls the canal now?

Materials:

paper
pencil
reference books
Internet (optional)

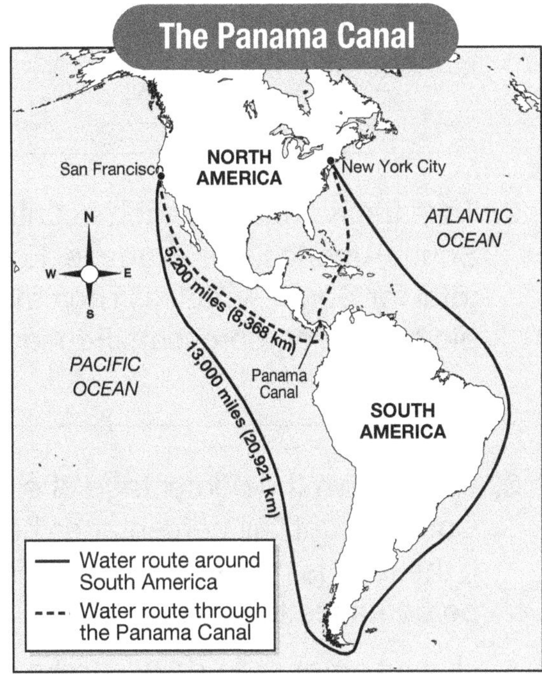

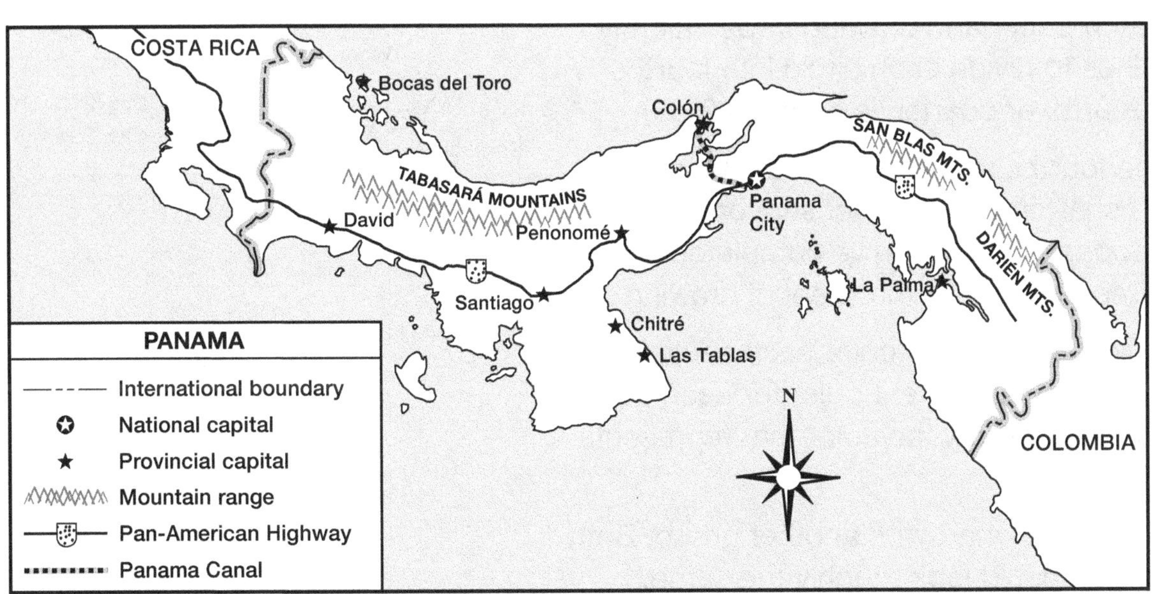

Make a Pie Chart

South America is home to a vast assortment of wildlife. Unfortunately, many species are endangered. Work with a group to create a pie chart based on the information presented in the map below.

Materials:

paper

pencil

calculator

compass

drawing paper

colored pencils

Directions

1. Add the numbers of endangered species in each country to find the total for South America. What is the total?

2. Take the number for each country shown on the map and divide it by the total for South America. For example, Ecuador has 23 endangered species. Divide 23 by the total for South America. Then multiply by 100. The product is the percentage of the pie chart that represents Ecuador. What is that percentage?

3. Write down the percentage of endangered species for each country on the map. Continue until all percentages have been calculated. Then add up the percentages. If the total is more or less than 100% (due to estimating), adjust some of the percentages to reach 100%.

4. Use a compass to draw a large circle on a sheet of scratch paper and drawing paper. Lightly draw lines to divide each circle into fourths (each fourth, or quarter, is equal to 25%).

5. Use the fourths as a guide to help you divide the pie chart into the proper sections on the scratch paper. Once you've completed the pie chart, reproduce it on the sheet of drawing paper.

6. Use colored pencils to color each section of the pie chart. Use a different color for each country. Make a key to show the color that represents each country.

7. Share your pie chart with another group. Both pie charts should look roughly the same.

Name _______________________________ Date _______________

Perform a Song

One of the world's most spectacular carnivals takes place in Rio de Janeiro, Brazil. It is called Carnival. Thousands of people attend Carnival to watch parades of performers dancing to the rhythmic Brazilian samba music. There are street performers, floats, costumes, and the most important event of Carnival—a fierce competition between rival samba schools to find out which one will receive the grand prize. Each school chooses a different theme, such as a special event, animal, or symbol. The samba music, floats, and costumes must relate to the theme. Plan a samba song and interpretive dance with your classmates.

Materials:

paper

pencil

Directions

1. Brainstorm a list of ideas with your group and write them down. Choose one as your theme for a song and interpretive dance.

2. Discuss the following questions:

   - Why is this theme important to us?

   - What do we want others to know about our theme?

   - How can we best express our theme?

3. As a group, write a song that expresses your theme. Your song may or may not rhyme. Clap out the rhythm and practice your song.

4. Create a dance that everyone will perform. Use movements and gestures to express what your song is about.

5. Perform your samba song and interpretive dance for the class.

Rio de Janeiro, Brazil

Create a Pottery Design

Ecuador is known for its beautiful pottery, rich in symbols and geometric design. Create your own geometric pottery design.

Directions

1. Sketch a large pot on a sheet of drawing paper. Make sure it is big enough to decorate.

2. Create a geometric design and lightly draw it on the pot. Use your design as a guide for cutting out the shapes from construction paper.

3. Glue the shapes onto the drawing of the pot.

4. When you have finished, present your pot to the class. Explain why you chose the pattern and what it means to you.

Materials:

construction paper

drawing paper

pencil

scissors

glue stick

paper

Name _________________________________   Date _______________

Catalog Plants and Animals

Scientists travel to tropical rainforests, like the ones in South America, to catalog and study plants and animals. Just like a scientist, you can study the plants and animals in your surroundings.

<table>
<tr><td>

Materials:

10 index cards

clipboard

outdoor area

pencil

magnifying glass
  (optional)

reference books

Internet (optional)

</td></tr>
</table>

Directions

1. Take five index cards, a pencil and a clipboard and go outside. Look for five interesting plants, animals, or insects to study.

2. Observe each one and draw a picture of it on the blank side of an index card. Try to add as much detail as possible.

3. On the lined side of the index card, write down the location of the plant or animal and a brief description of what it looks like. If you are studying an insect or an animal, also write down how it moves and what it does.

4. Bring your completed index cards back inside. Use reference books or the Internet to research five interesting plants, animals, or insects from South America.

5. Create five index cards about the South American plants, animals, or insects you chose. Draw pictures of the plant, animal, or insect on the front of the cards. On the back of the cards, write brief descriptions.

6. Share your findings with the class. Discuss similarities and differences between the plants, animals, and insects in your region with those from South America.

7. Give your index cards to your teacher so they can be displayed as part of a class catalog.

Draw a Diagram of the Catatumbo Lightning

Did you know that the world's largest lightning storm produces more than 1 million bolts of lightning per year? This gigantic lightning storm occurs in Venezuela near the Catatumbo River and Lake Maracaibo. It is known as the Catatumbo Lightning. With a group, research the Catatumbo Lightning and draw a diagram to explain what causes this phenomenon.

Materials:
reference books
Internet (optional)
poster board
markers
paper
pencil

Directions

1. Use reference books or the Internet to research the Catatumbo Lightning. Take notes and include the following information for your diagram:

Andes Mountains	methane gas	Lake Maracaibo	Catatumbo River
electrical charges	bog/swamp	vertical clouds	thunderstorms

2. Sketch a diagram on a sheet of paper that includes the eight terms listed above.

3. Use markers to reproduce the sketch on the poster board. Have all members label the parts of the diagram and write phrases that tell what is happening.

4. Present your poster to the class and take turns telling about what is happening in the diagram. Display your poster in the classroom.

Multiple Intelligences G4–6, SV 9780547625744

Design Paper People

The people of South America wear a variety of traditional clothing. Suppose you were visiting South America. What kind of clothing would you want to wear? Would you wear a Peruvian montera or perhaps a Chilean chamanto? Make a paper person and design some South American clothing.

Directions

1. Draw and cut out a paper person on a sheet of cardboard. Use reference books or the Internet to research several South American countries and take note of the traditional clothing.

2. Choose one or two types of clothing that you would like to make.

3. Place your paper person on a sheet of drawing paper and trace around the body.

4. Draw and color the traditional clothing on the outline you just drew. Draw tabs so that you will be able to fasten the clothes to your paper person.

5. Cut out the clothing and the tabs. Dress your paper person in traditional clothing. Fold the tabs to make the clothes stay on.

6. Show your paper person to a partner. See if your partner can guess what country your person is from based on the clothing.

Materials:
- reference books
- Internet (optional)
- cardboard
- pencil
- drawing paper
- colored pencils
- scissors

Multiple Intelligences G4–6, SV 9780547625744

Create a South American Travel Brochure

Create a travel brochure to convince others to visit South America

Directions

1. Choose a South American city to write about. You can use a map or globe to help you choose one.

2. Use reference books or the Internet to conduct research to find out about the place you chose. Takes notes as you find the answers to questions like these:

   - What is the temperature like?

   - How do people dress?

   - What kinds of landforms exist?

   - What makes this city special?

3. Fold your drawing paper into thirds.

4. Use the information you gathered from your research to write about the city. Include drawings and make your travel brochure interesting and eye-catching so people will want to visit the city.

5. Exchange travel brochures with a partner. Read one another's brochures.

Materials:

drawing paper

paper

map or globe

reference books

Internet (optional)

pencil

crayons

Make a Travel Invitation

Make a travel invitation to ask a friend to join you on a trip to South America

Materials:

pencil
colored pencils
drawing paper

Directions

1. Suppose you were going on a trip to South America. It would be fun to go with a friend.

2. Make a travel invitation like the one below. On the back, write down a list of things your friend should pack, such as a hat, a pair of binoculars, or a swimsuit.

3. Decorate and color your invitation. Then exchange invitations with a classmate.

4. Tell your classmate one thing you would like to do on vacation in South America.

What: _______________________________

Date: _______________________________

Time: _______________________________

Where: _______________________________

Perform a South American Chant

Write and perform a chant that tells about the fun things you can do in South America.

Materials:

paper
pencil
reference books
Internet (optional)

Directions

1. Choose a few places in South America that interest you. Use reference books or the Internet to research fun things to do there.

2. Use your ideas to help you write a chant. An example has been provided.

   Argentina, Venezuela,
   and Guyana too,
   many beaches, many places,
   there's a lot to do!

3. Say the words aloud as you clap the beat or tap your foot to the rhythm.

4. Practice your chant and then perform it for others.

Multiple Intelligences G4–6, SV 9780547625744

Answer Key

Page 9

1. Tallest building: Willis Tower; located in Chicago; completed construction in 1974; 1,450 feet high; 110 floors.
   Second tallest building: Trump International Hotel and Tower; located in Chicago; completed construction in 2009; 1,389 feet high; 98 floors.
   Third tallest building: Empire State Building; located in New York City; completed construction in 1931; 1,250 feet high; 102 floors.

Page 16

1. 209 feet
2. 63 rows
3. 627 plants
4. 39,501 plants

Page 26

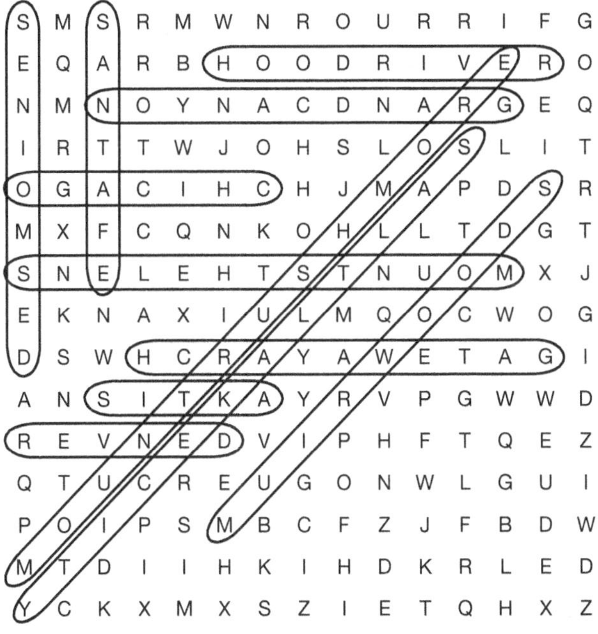

1. IL
2. MO
3. SD
4. UT
5. CO
6. AZ
7. WA
8. NM
9. IA
10. OR
11. CA
12. AK

Page 38

a. colonies on the left; England on the right

b. British Parliament; a whip and strings;Great Britain was crippled during the French and Indian War; The British flag

c. a group of colonists; they are puppets without control; Britain; they are protesting and they are struggling to get away

d. After the French and Indian War, Great Britain's economy was injured. Great Britain could barely support itself economically, so it heavily taxed the colonists. The government used threats of force to make the colonists obey and pay taxes; yes; Great Britain is portrayed in a bad way; a British cartoonist would not portray Great Britain in this way

Page 69

Mount Vesuvius /Italy
Old Rauma /Finland
Red Square /Russia
Grand Place /Belgium

The Golden Tower /Spain
The Acropolis /Greece
Jungfrau /Switzerland
Marko's Fortress /Macedonia

The Louvre /France
Stonehenge /England
Loch Ness /Scotland
Myvatn /Iceland

Page 73

1. Bangladesh; 100 times
2. Bangladesh; 2 times
3. population; Bangladesh is about 100 times larger on the cartogram than it is on a land area map.
4. answers will vary

Page 100

1. 239
2. about 10%

Answer Key
Multiple Intelligences G4–6, SV 9780547625744

Europe

Reykjavik
ICELAND
Arctic Circle
60°N
Norwegian Sea
SWEDEN
FINLAND
NORWAY
Oslo
Helsinki
Stockholm
Tallinn
ESTONIA
North Sea
Baltic Sea
LEGEND
National boundary
National capital
km 0   200   400
mi 0   200   400
IRELAND
Dublin
Riga
LATVIA
Moscow
50°N
UNITED KINGDOM
Copenhagen
LITHUANIA
DENMARK
Vilnius
Minsk
RUSSIA
London
NETHERLANDS
Berlin
RUSSIA
BELARUS
Amsterdam
Warsaw
Brussels
GERMANY
POLAND
Kiev
ATLANTIC
BELGIUM
Luxembourg
Prague
UKRAINE
OCEAN
Paris
LUX.
CZECH
REPUBLIC
SLOVAKIA
1
Vienna
Bratislava
MOLDOVA
Bay of
Bern
AUSTRIA
Budapest
Biscay
FRANCE
SWITZ.
Vaduz
HUNGARY
Chisinau
Ljubljana
ROMANIA
40°N
SLOVENIA
Zagreb
ANDORRA
Monte
CROATIA
Bucharest
Carlo
2
Sarajevo
Black Sea
PORTUGAL
Andorra
3
Belgrade
Madrid
ITALY
Adriatic Sea
5
BULGARIA
Lisbon
MONACO
Rome
6
SPAIN
Podgorica
Sofia
Skopje
Tirana
4
10°W
ASIA
ALBANIA
GREECE
Aegean Sea
Strait of Gibraltar
Athens
1. LIECHTENSTEIN
2. SAN MARINO
3. BOSNIA AND
   HERZEGOVINA
AFRICA
4. MACEDONIA
Valletta
5. SERBIA
MALTA
Mediterranean Sea
6. MONTENEGRO
0°
10°E
20°E
30°E

110

Africa

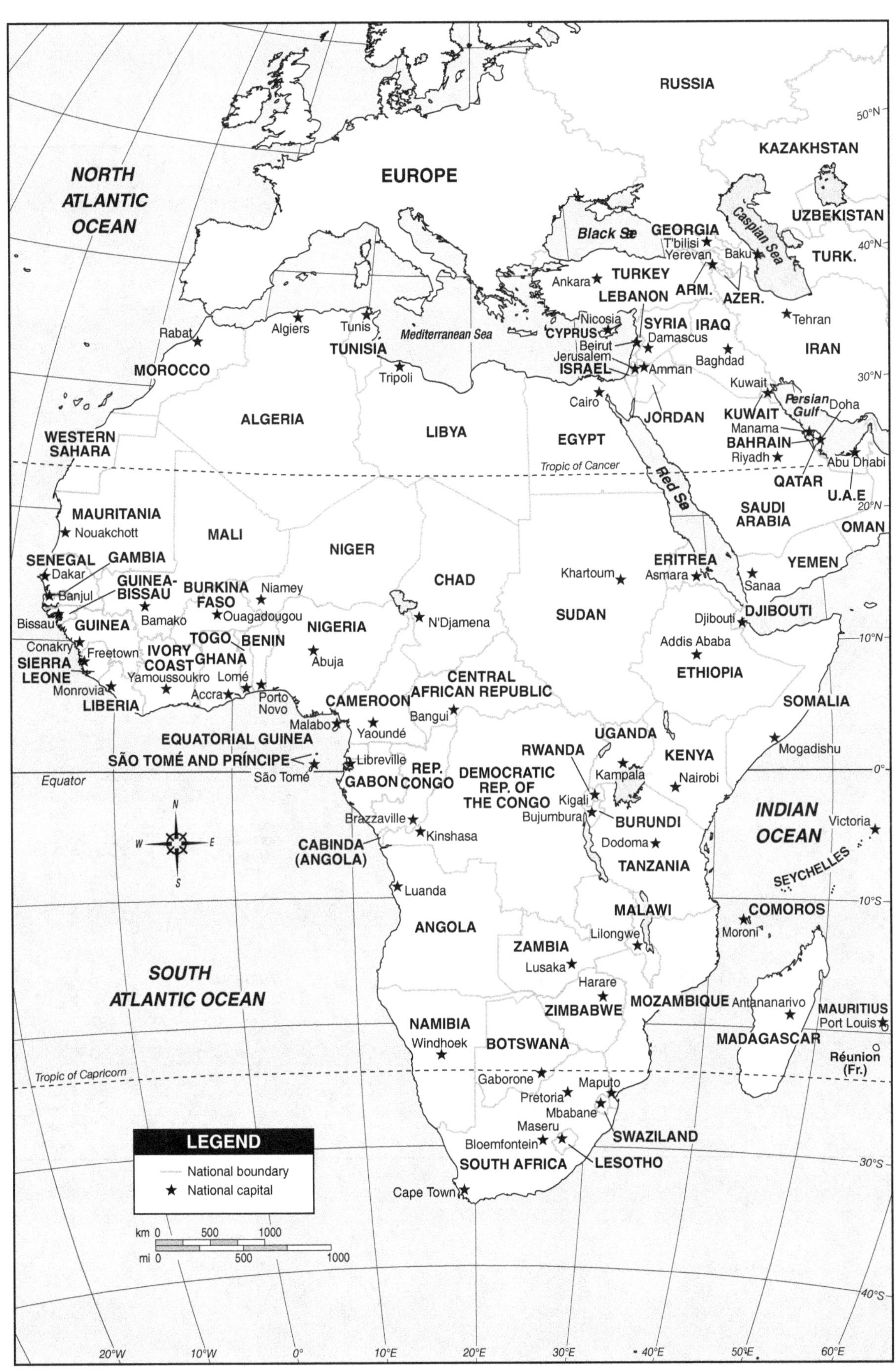

Maps
Multiple Intelligences G4–6, SV 9780547625744

Asia and the South Pacific

Multiple Intelligences G4–6, SV 9780547625744

Eastern Hemisphere

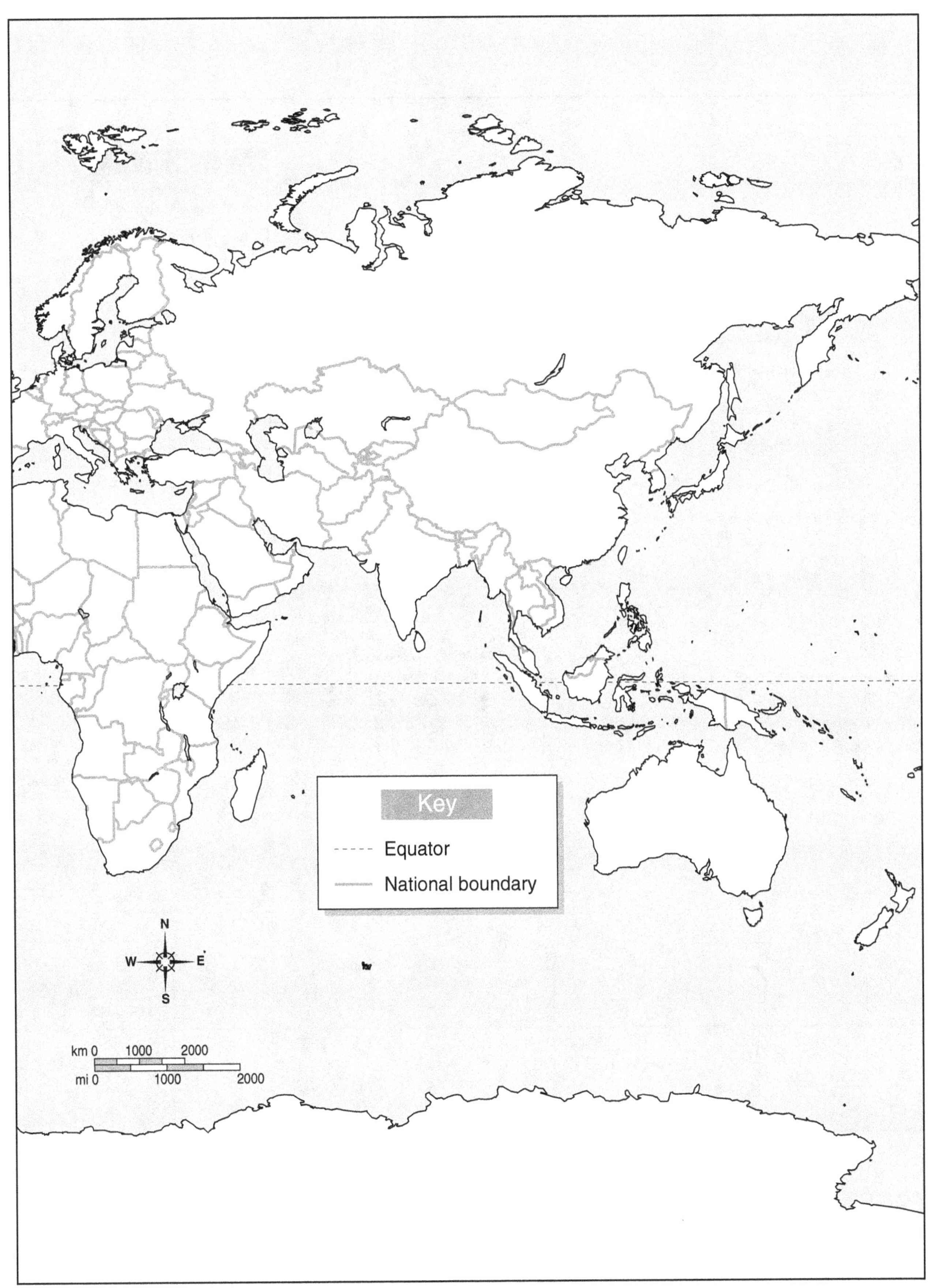

Australia and South Pacific

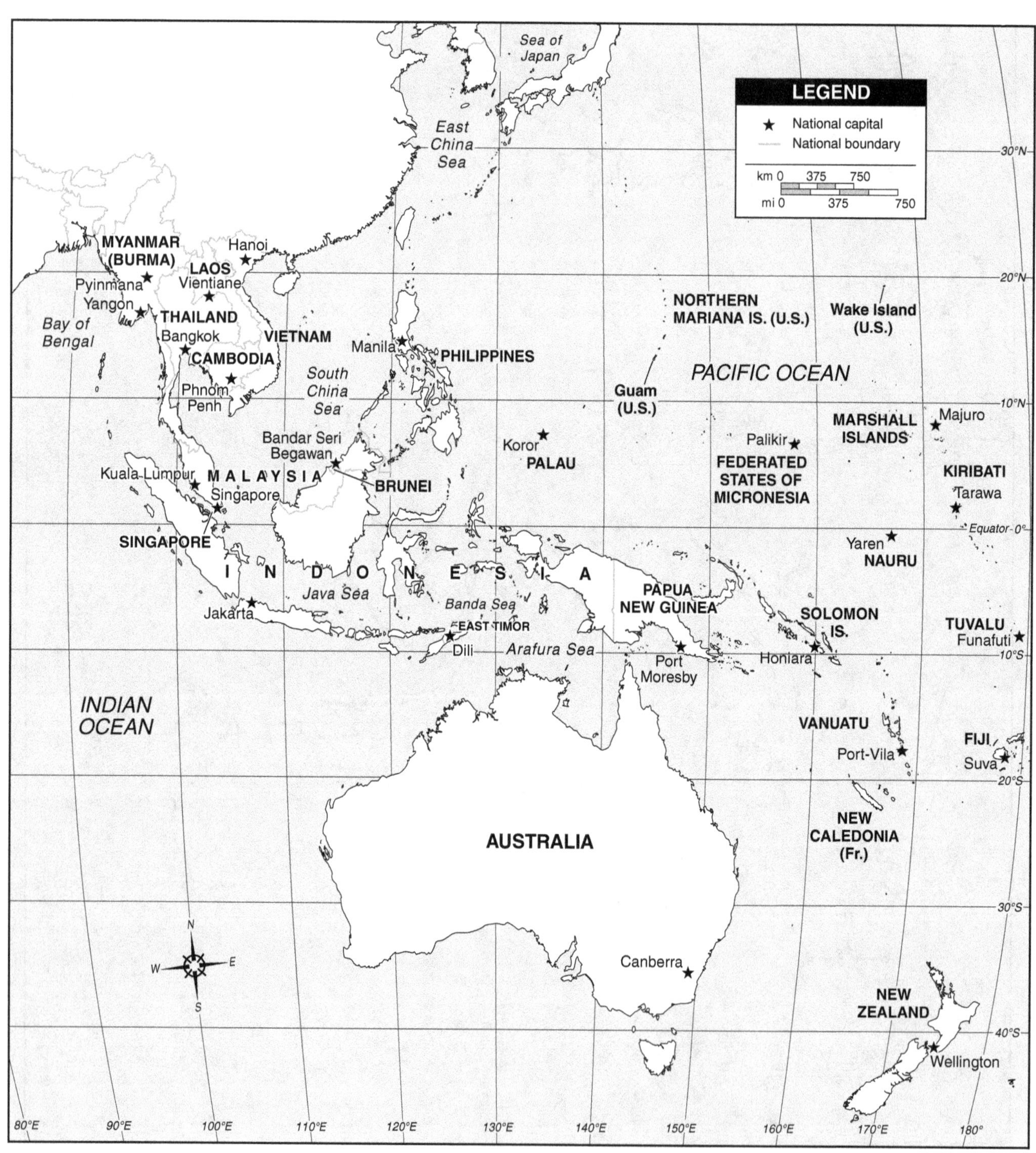

Multiple Intelligences G4–6, SV 9780547625744

North America

The United States of America

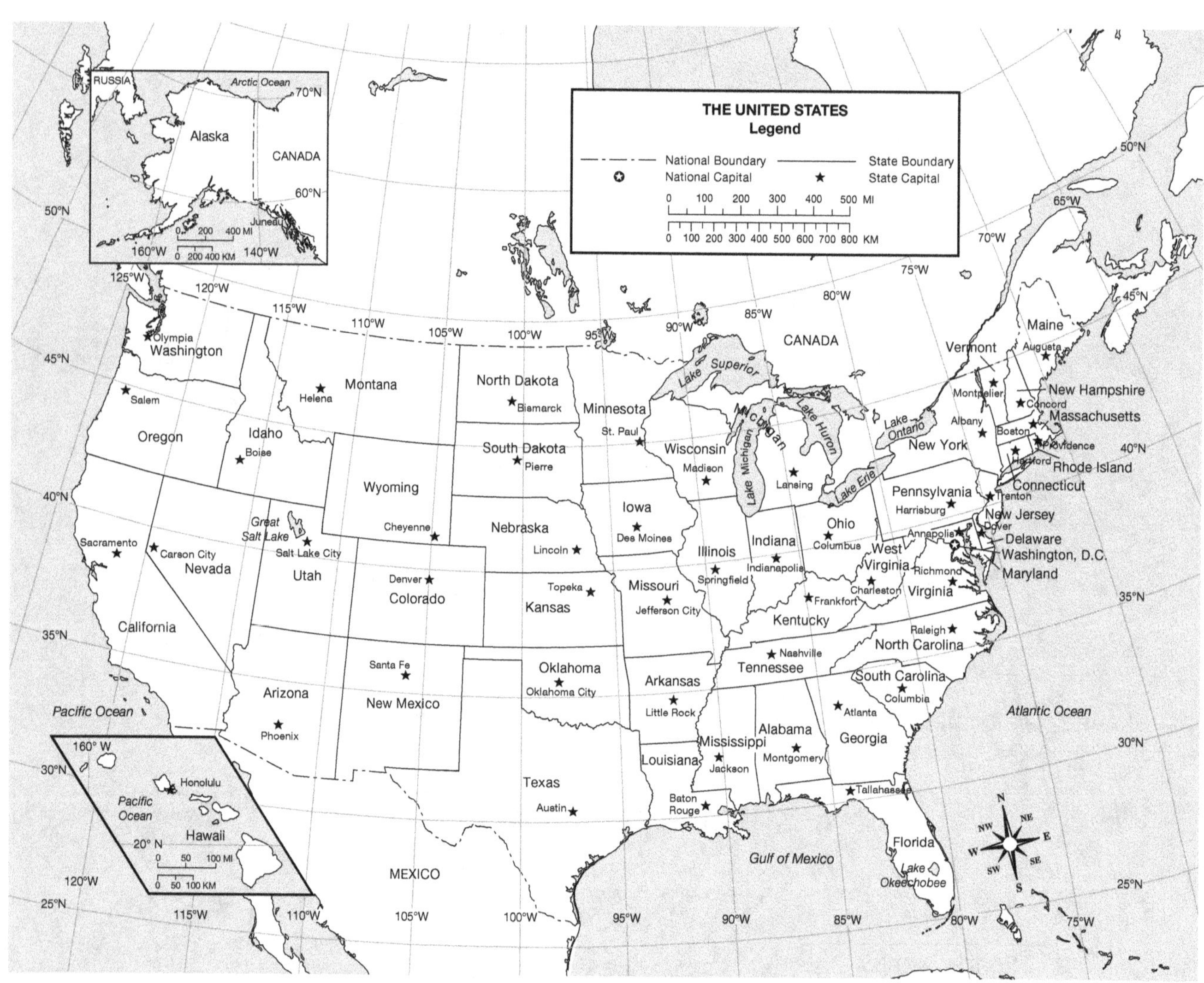

Central America

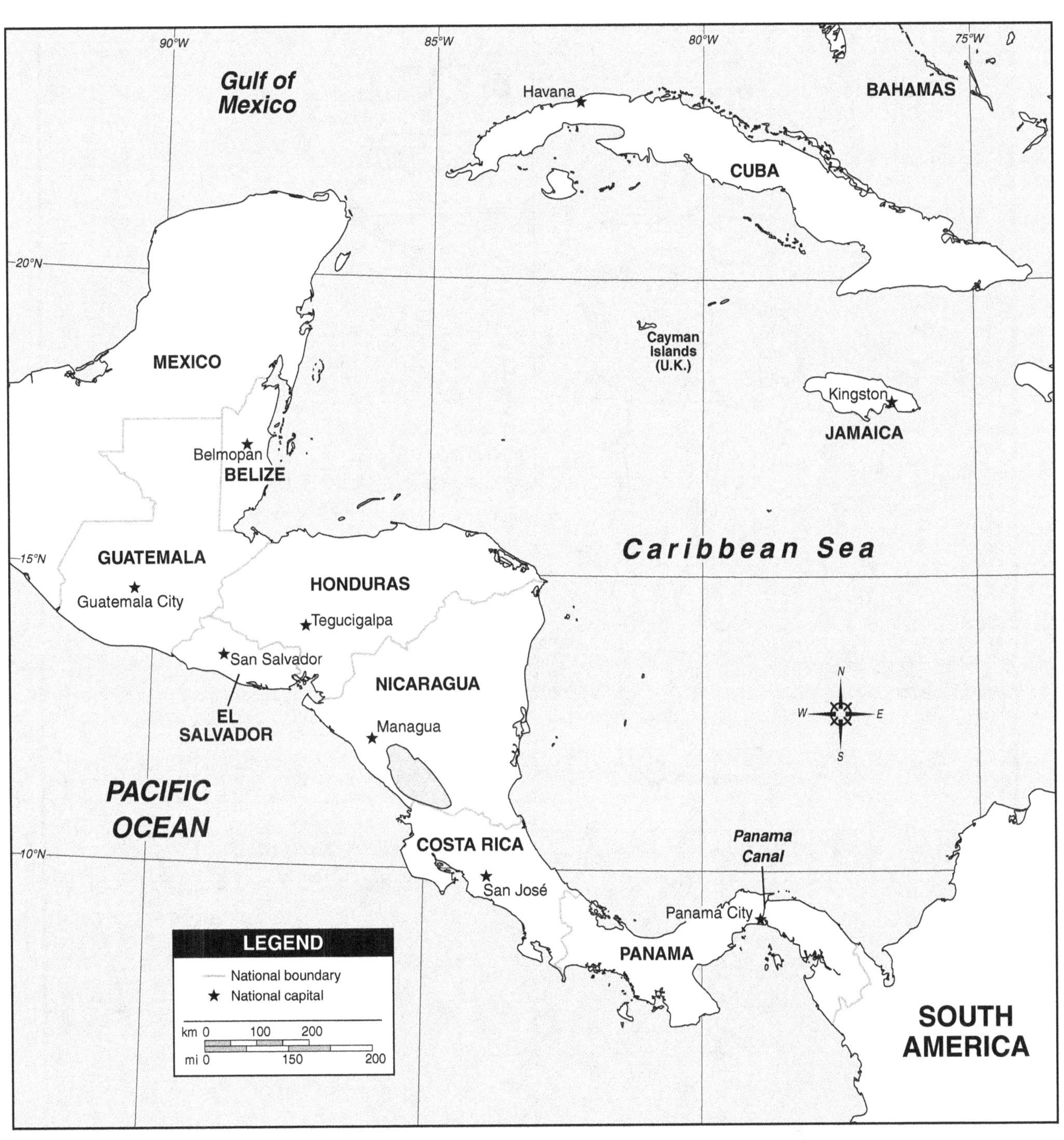

Multiple Intelligences G4–6, SV 9780547625744

South America